Images of **Beckett**

Images of Beckett sets John Haynes' unique repertoire of photographs of Beckett's dramatic opus alongside three newly written essays by Beckett's biographer and friend, James Knowlson. Haynes captures images of Beckett's work in progress and performance and includes hitherto unseen portraits of Beckett himself. Haynes was privileged to be present at the Royal Court Theatre in London when Beckett directed his own plays. Among the 75 photographs are compositions that include the leading interpreters of the plays. Knowlson's first essay combines a verbal portrait of Beckett with a personal memoir of the writer; the second considers the influence of paintings that Beckett loved or admired on his theatrical imagery; the third offers a detailed, often first-hand, account of Beckett's work as a director of his own plays. The essays are the result of personal conversations with Beckett and attendance at rehearsals. They provide a unique glimpse into the world of one of the theatre's most influential and enduring playwrights.

JOHN HAYNES' previous book *Taking the Stage*, with an introduction by Lindsay Anderson, has become a classic of theatre photography. He was privileged to work alongside Samuel Beckett when he was directing his plays at the Royal Court in the 1970s, when John was photographer in residence. Haynes continues to work with the leading directors and actors of British contemporary theatre.

JAMES KNOWLSON is the author of the major Beckett biography, *Damned to Fame. The Life of Samuel Beckett* (Bloomsbury, 1996). He is also the author of ten other books on or editions of Beckett. He was a personal friend of Samuel Beckett for twenty years.

Images of
Beckett

Photographs by **John Haynes**

Text by **James Knowlson**

CAMBRIDGE
UNIVERSITY PRESS

PUBLISHED BY THE PRESS SYNDICATE OF THE UNIVERSITY OF CAMBRIDGE
The Pitt Building, Trumpington Street, Cambridge CB2 1RP, United Kingdom

CAMBRIDGE UNIVERSITY PRESS
The Edinburgh Building, Cambridge, CB2 2RU, UK
40 West 20th Street, New York, NY 10011–4211, USA
477 Williamstown Road, Port Melbourne, VIC 3207, Australia
Ruiz de Alarcón 13, 28014 Madrid, Spain
Dock House, The Waterfront, Cape Town 8001, South Africa

http://www.cambridge.org

First published 2003

Printed in the United Kingdom at the University Press, Cambridge

Typeface Quadraat regular 10/14pt.   *System* LaTeX 2$_\varepsilon$ [TB]

A catalogue record for this book is available from the British Library

ISBN 0 521 82258 0 hardback

To Jane and Elizabeth

Contents

Preface and acknowledgements

This book has its origins in the admiration I felt over a period of many years for John Haynes' photographs of Samuel Beckett and his plays. The idea evolved further with John's appointment as Annenberg Fellow at my home university, the University of Reading. This post was made possible by a generous award from the Annenberg Foundation, set up in the USA by the late Walter Annenberg. The fellowship was established through the good offices of his grand-daughter, Lauren Ariel Bon. I thank her and the trustees most warmly here for their support.

During his year as a fellow, an exhibition of Haynes' photographs was assembled by John and Stephen Buckley and exhibited as Samuel Beckett on Stage, first in Reading, then in London and Berlin. This revealed what a rich archive he had of Beckett photographs (many previously unseen) and I felt that these ought to be more widely disseminated for others to appreciate and enjoy. We agreed to work together and this book of essays and photographs is the fruit of our collaboration. We have not attempted to make the photographs directly illustrate the texts, but have preferred to set up echoes from one to the other.

Extracts from Beckett's writings, published or unpublished, appear with the kind permission of Edward Beckett and the Beckett Estate and his writings in English are quoted by kind permission of Faber & Faber Ltd, Calder Publications and Grove Press, who hold the copyrights to his published work.

I am also very grateful to the National Humanities Center in Research Triangle Park, North Carolina, for appointing me to the Gladys Krieble Delmas Fellowship. I was able to complete the essays there and thank Karen Carroll for her editorial help. As always, my wife, Elizabeth, helped me with the various stages of the manuscript.

John Haynes would like to thank William Gaskill, Jocelyn Herbert, Anthony Page and the Royal Court Theatre in London, the Gate Theatre in Dublin, the Peter Hall Company and the actors, directors, designers and lighting designers who made these pictures possible.

Both of us would like to thank the Beckett International Foundation at the University of Reading and our editor, Victoria Cooper, the designer, Stephanie Thelwell and the production department at Cambridge University Press.

James Knowlson

Illustrations

PLATES

Note: Every effort has been made to obtain permission to use copyright materials; the publishers apologise for any omissions and would welcome these being brought to their attention.

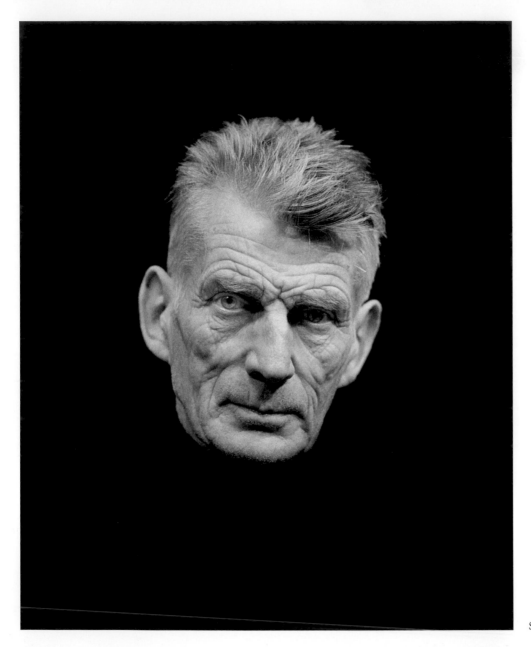

Samuel Beckett, 1973

A portrait of Beckett

Samuel Beckett was undoubtedly one of the 'stars' of twentieth-century literature and theatre. After more than two decades of obscurity, he became equally famous in both French and English, translating himself regularly from one language into the other. His four major plays, *Waiting for Godot* and *Endgame* (first written in French), *Krapp's Last Tape* and *Happy Days* (first written in English) and his novel trilogy, *Molloy, Malone Dies* and *The Unnamable* (first written in French), with their translations into dozens of languages, made him a key figure on the world literary stage. He was awarded several prestigious international awards, the most distinguished of which were the International Publishers' Prize in 1961 (shared with Jorge Luis Borges) and the Nobel Prize for Literature in 1969. Few writers have been more celebrated during their lifetime; yet he disliked the trappings of fame. His craggy, deeply furrowed face became instantly recognisable; yet he hated to be recognised. He loathed all forms of self-exposure or self-promotion and gave a polite but firm 'no' whenever he was asked to give an interview or to speak in public or on the radio and television. As a result, he retained an exceptional air of mystery and myths naturally accrued around him. Many persisted long after his death.

The first and most natural of these myths was that he was a latter-day hermit, living a reclusive existence in his seventh-floor apartment on the boulevard Saint-Jacques in Paris. He certainly loved silence, solitude and peace. Visiting Germany in 1936, he wrote in his personal diary of 'the absurd beauty of being alone',[1] and, after a long, solitary walk in the Tiergarten in Berlin – an area vast enough to find oneself alone in even today – he wrote: 'How I ADORE solitude'[2] (the capital letters were Beckett's own). It was not just a love of solitude for its own sake either. Silence and solitude were, he recognised, vital for his writing. 'Down into the now friendly dark',[3] he wrote, as he plunged into creating the extraordinarily dense, innovative prose text that was to become *Comment c'est* (*How It Is*) in the remote tranquillity of his country cottage at Ussy-sur-Marne. A tall, forbidding wall of ugly, grey, utilitarian breeze blocks surrounded the austere little property, preventing anyone from looking in from the road and

restricting to some extent his own view. The wall was a visible sign of how much he detested intrusions into his private life.

His social life in the city was, however, often exceptionally hectic. He complained to a friend that 'being in Paris is mostly siege fever'.[4] He had, literally, hundreds of friends or acquaintances, from many professions and many countries – painters, musicians, directors, writers, academics – and a surprising number of really close friends. Someone once commented to me: 'I've never met so many people dashing off to Paris by plane or by train to see this so-called hermit!' Consulting his appointment diaries for the last twenty years of his life, while writing Beckett's authorised biography, I was amazed at how he managed to fit in as much work as he did, in view of the many distractions that he had. In Paris, he would often have two, three, sometimes even four appointments a day, for weeks on end, meeting relatives, friends, collaborators, and publishers, as well as many more casual visitors. He devoted a lot of his time to answering a huge correspondence, writing most of the letters himself, usually by hand.

He adopted a number of ingenious strategies for coping with the less pleasurable pressures that fame exerted on him, especially after the award of the Nobel Prize for Literature. In the seventies and eighties, for instance, he answered the telephone only in the morning between eleven o'clock and twelve noon. Before that, it had been between ten and eleven. He bought a telephone with a red on–off button, which, when switched off, blocked incoming calls. (Ironically for someone who was so enamoured of silence and so jealous of his privacy, the telephone is now displayed in a glass case in the Writers' Museum in Dublin.) Friends knew that, except by letter, telegram or pneumatique, they could only reach him during that one hour of the day. Sometimes he deliberately did not switch on the telephone at all: 'I haven't been opening the phone regularly for some time', he wrote to a London friend in 1972.[5]

His appointments were mostly arranged by letter, and were usually made well in advance. Non-personal letters were dealt with by a quick comment

(Left) Samuel Beckett, 1973

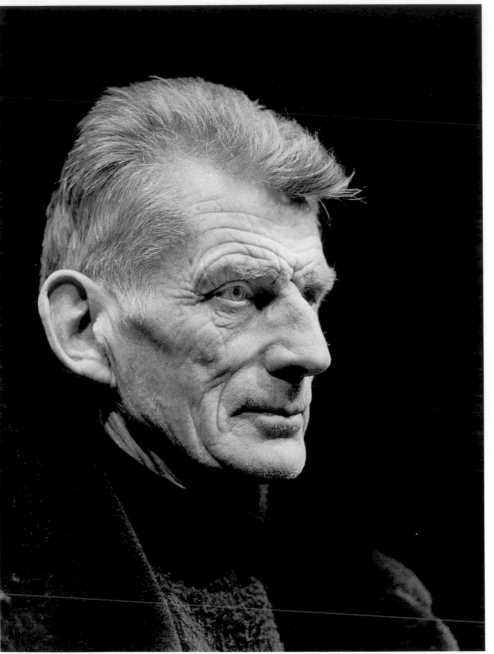

that he added to the foot or on the back of the letter itself, or, alternatively, by a system of symbols agreed with his French publisher, Jérôme Lindon's secretary at Les Editions de Minuit. She then answered these letters for him, often with a number of standard replies: 'Mr Beckett never gives interviews'; 'Mr Beckett does not read theses and manuscripts about his work'; 'Mr Beckett is away in the country.' The last comment was not always true, but it provided a plausible excuse and was often the only way for him to carve out sizeable slices of time for his writing.

These efforts to achieve a calm, untroubled existence in Paris were, however, doomed to failure – primarily on account of his own generous nature. He simply could not bring himself to say 'no' to friends who were travelling to the capital in the hope of seeing him. So he would rush in from the country especially to meet them for lunch or for drinks, leaving the house at 5.30 in the morning in his modest little grey Citroën Deux-Chevaux to catch the 6 o'clock train from the nearby town of La Ferté-sous-Jouarre. He was often sent recorded packages. If he happened to be out at the time of delivery, he then had to queue at the post office to extricate material, which, most of the time, he did not want; ' PLEASE don't send it to me recorded delivery', he would plead plaintively. At home he had no secretarial help, since neither he nor his French wife, Suzanne, could bear to have someone coming regularly into their apartment. For a short

Samuel Beckett, 1973

time, his old friend, A. J. ('Con') Leventhal, who retired from Trinity College and came over from Dublin to live in Paris, tried to help him with his business affairs. But Beckett was never a delegator and, in any case, business problems could not always be resolved by his publishers and literary or dramatic agents without involving, or at least consulting, him personally.

His work created its own wash, which threatened to become a tidal wave, ready to swamp all future writing. Even so, the number of late manuscripts that have 'Paris' as the place in which they were written, shows the degree of concentration that he was able to bring to his work, whenever he was allowed. But his appointment diaries also reveal that he deliberately carved out large slabs of time – page after page of white space in his diaries – when he would make no appointments at all. At such times he would take himself off alone to Ussy and immerse himself in his beloved silence, to write or simply to recover from the stresses and strains of too much socialising, often, it should be said, of too much wine or whiskey. When the world-wide success of *Waiting for Godot* eventually made money no object, he would go away on holiday for weeks on end, usually with Suzanne, to quiet places out of season, such as Sardinia, the Vale of Aosta, Madeira, Porto Santo, Malta, Greece and the Greek islands, Zell-am-See, Kitzbühel, or Tangiers. Even then, he regularly took some piece of writing or self-translation away with him.

Laying huge store by his work meant that Beckett's frustrations were much greater whenever his writing appeared to be leading nowhere. He fumed against people and circumstances, when the problem sometimes lay in an absence of inspiration or in his own too ready willingness to say 'yes' to the demands made on his time. Early in 1977, for example, he wrote, 'Attempts to get going on new work [are] fruitless'[6] and 'writing [is] in the doldrums';[7] 'with me endless interruptions, endless mail, no possibility of work. Submerged. See no way out.'[8] In January 1983, in a period of deep gloom, he wrote to Larry Shainberg: 'such inertia and void as never before. I remember an entry in Kafka's Diary. "Gardening. No hope for the future." At least he could garden. There must be words for it. I don't expect ever to find them.'[9]

The cry became a familiar one. But after the age of 70 the feeling that time was running out for him made him more desperate than ever before. 'Damned to fame', he wrote to me in 1981, quoting Alexander Pope's words in *The Dunciad* and lamenting the fact that a festival that was being organised to honour him on his seventy-fifth birthday would impinge on both his time and his privacy.[10] 'I dread the year now upon us', he wrote to his friend, the English stage designer, Jocelyn Herbert, 'and all the fuss in store for me here [in Paris], as if it were my centenary. I'll make myself scarce while it lasts, where I don't know. Perhaps the Great Wall of China, crouch behind it till the coast is clear.'[11]

Beckett was very reticent in discussing his own work. He made no attempt whatever to explain it, when a journalist (with whom he might exceptionally agree to have a friendly chat, but never an interview), a critic, or even a friend asked him what it meant. This arose partly out of a natural reluctance to dispel the mystery that, for him, surrounded a work of art. It also stemmed from his awareness that, as the author, he was, as he once put it, 'the worm at the core of the apple', unable to view the entire apple from the outside.

As a consequence of this reticence, a second myth developed that he was difficult, uncooperative and wilfully obscurantist. Nothing could have

Samuel Beckett, 1973

(*Left*) Alan Howard and Ben Kingsley in *Waiting for Godot*, 1997

been further from the truth. He was invariably helpful, for example, to actors with whom he was working. But his suggestions were practical, detailed and down-to-earth, confined to what they needed to speak their lines or perform their moves or gestures. He never entered into discussions with them about philosophical issues or even questions of psychological motivation. In private conversations, he was much more at ease discussing the practical problems of a particular production or the strengths of an individual actor or actress than he was in elucidating the themes or discussing the imagery of his plays. With academics who were writing books and articles on his work, he was also remarkably cooperative, providing them with information, mostly of a bibliographical or textual nature, since, again, he did not trespass into areas of meaning and interpretation.

There were, nonetheless, occasions when, privately, he could be quite revealing about his art, his approach to theatre and his practice as a writer. While dining with him once in Paris, for instance, I remember referring to the musical rhythms of his play, *Krapp's Last Tape*, and wondering if, like Gustave Flaubert in what the great French novelist used to describe as his *gueuloire*, he read his words out aloud. 'I do', agreed Beckett and went on to quote the passage in which Krapp is lying with the girl in the punt, adding: 'if you take a single syllable out of those lines, you destroy the sound of the lapping of the water on the side of the boat'. His comment was followed by an embarrassed laugh, as if he had somehow committed an indiscretion.

On another occasion – and the example is typical of how Beckett came to make such observations – we had been discussing the difficulty that he was experiencing in translating his play, *That Time*, into French. 'There is a problem with the title to begin with', he said. 'After all *That Time* means both "the time when" and "that Time" in the wider sense. How ever do you render both?' For his published French translation, he had to settle on *Cette fois*, thereby missing the wider Proustian allusion to Time as 'that double-headed monster of damnation and salvation', about which he had written in his early

(*Right*) John Hurt in *Krapp's Last Tape*, 1999

study of Proust.[12] On a later occasion, he explained to me that he had found it even harder to translate his play, *A Piece of Monologue*, into French and had been forced to 'cut things out because I simply can't render in French certain sounds made by the voice in English'. He was clearly thinking of the plosive sound of the word *Birth*, the 'rip-word' referred to by the speaker. So he explained that, for this reason, the French version had turned out to be shorter than the English original.

Before undertaking to write his biography, I scarcely ever made notes after my meetings with Beckett but, on one occasion, a *dîner à deux* on his seventy-seventh birthday in 1983, I did. Part of the evening found us talking about the shorter plays that he had recently written or translated. Of his 1980 play, *Rockaby*, Beckett commented: 'It's the same woman as in *Footfalls*. She has just gone a stage further. Perhaps she's tired of "revolving it all".' And he pointed out that he had asked the actress Billie Whitelaw not to perform the two plays together on the same programme in Tokyo on account of the closeness of their parentage. I had been very intrigued by his television play, *Quad*, in which four figures move frenetically across a square from its corners in intricate patterns of rapid movement. So, at the same dinner, puzzled by the significance of the centre, the 'danger zone' that all the figures carefully, even obsessively avoid, I asked him whether this taboo area could be related to the Taoist 'quiet centre'. 'No – at least that was not my intention', he replied. He wanted to emphasise rather, he said, 'the constant agitation of man's existence', thereby leaving his intention as to the middle area of the square totally unexplained. A second version, *Quad II*, had been filmed, almost as an afterthought, he added, at the Süddeutscher Rundfunk studios in Stuttgart, at a slower speed and in black and white, because it took place 'a thousand years on'.

It was fascinating, as well as hugely entertaining, to spend entire evenings in Beckett's company. Sometimes this was because of its very ordinariness. For someone who guarded his own privacy so jealously, Beckett was intensely curious about the private lives of others, and enjoyed a good

(*Left*) Samuel Beckett, 1973

gossip as much as anyone else. He often talked of friends you had in common and of your own family. He had a good memory but, in addition, he adopted the neat little trick of writing down children's names alongside the names of his friends and acquaintances in his address book, so that, flatteringly, he always appeared unusually well informed about their wives and their families.

He often talked about sport. Throughout his life, it remained one of his principal interests. The sports were not always those normally associated with Beckett either. Boxing was one of these. He quite often used to listen to radio commentaries on championship fights. Rugby football, cricket and golf in particular retained his interest, even into his eighties. As a young man, he was a fair tennis player, a good cricketer and golfer and a fine centre three-quarter at rugby, playing for the Ecole Normale in Paris, as well as, earlier, for his old school, the Portora Royal School in Enniskillen. In the 1950s he used to go to the Roland Garros stadium to watch international tennis. He had an excellent touch at billiards. On his one and only visit to the USA in 1964, he went to the Shea baseball stadium in New York with Richard Seaver and Judith Schmidt, following the game with the unfeigned interest of a true sportsman. When he opened an English newspaper, he invariably turned first to the sports results; in French, he read the sports paper, *L'Equipe*, as well as, for current

Patrick Magee in *Endgame*, 1976

Samuel Beckett, 1973

affairs, first *Combat* or *L'Humanité*, then, later on in his life, *Libération*, all left-wing newspapers.

When he was over in London during the summer to help with productions of his plays, a lunch-time drink in a local pub would find him with his eyes glued to a television set, particularly when a Test Match was being played between England and Australia. Cricket and rugby were among our regular topics of conversation. Other friends spoke to him about golf. If you were visiting him in Paris, or when he was directing his plays in London, you soon learned never to try to make an appointment for a Saturday afternoon, when he would be totally engrossed in the radio or television commentaries on international rugby or other sports. That period of the week was sacrosanct.

Chess was a lifetime passion with Beckett and found its way into several of his works.[13] He idolised Capablanca and Alekhin and had dozens of chess books in his library. He was an avid fan of the chess columns in *Le Monde* and played chess regularly for more than twenty years with his painter friend, Henri Hayden. The Surrealist painter and chess Grand Master, Marcel Duchamp, was, Beckett told me, much too good for him. Yet he said this with the quiet satisfaction of knowing that he had played against someone of that calibre.

Often, however, an evening with Beckett could be far from ordinary. I remember being elated on many occasions when he revealed the vast range of

his reading in European literature. This embraced far more than the authors he referred to as the 'old chestnuts': Dante, Shakespeare, Milton, Pascal, Racine, Dr Johnson, Goethe, Heine, W. B. Yeats, Synge and, selectively, Hölderlin.[14] I was fascinated, for instance, when, suddenly, as we spoke about his own late plays, he quoted by heart some lines from a little-known poem by the French Parnassian poet, José Maria de Heredia, about the Florentine sculptor and goldsmith, Benvenuto Cellini. 'Cellini, ignorant la foule, sur le Pont des Soupirs, ciselait sur le pommeau d'une dague le combat des Titans [Unmindful of the crowd, on the Bridge of Sighs, Cellini was chiselling on the pommel of a dagger the combat of the Titans].' 'I often feel like Cellini, you know', Beckett commented in a confidential tone, 'as I chisel away at my work.'[15] All of Beckett's friends have their own favourite examples of such moments of deeper insight into his real obsessions and most passionate and abiding interests – in painting, music and poetry. One recent memoir by Anne Atik, the wife of the painter Avigdor Arikha, is particularly fascinating on Beckett's tastes in literature and music and on the poetry that Beckett could recite by heart.[16]

With Beckett, as often happens with those who have wide-ranging intellectual and artistic interests, the personal tended to lead into more general issues, then back into the personal again. So, as he told me about how weary he had been

Billie Whitelaw in *Happy Days*, 1979

feeling over the past few weeks, he asked if I knew the poem by Heine in which the poet (whom Beckett loved) wrote of the 'grinding out of life', the 'old round'.[17] This led seamlessly into a revealing insight as to how he felt about old age in relation to his own writing. 'Between the weaknesses of childhood and the senility of age', he said, 'there lies all the nonsense of striving and searching for knowledge – this parabola. I always hoped though from an early age that old age offered a chance of seeing the essentials away from all the agitation of being.'[18] He went on to speak of the wonderful writings that Goethe and W. B. Yeats had produced in the final years of their lives and of how he had himself always associated old age with light and with the spirit. He felt deeply the need for spirit. 'It has been the malaise of our time', he said to Patrick Bowles. 'People are not in touch with their spirit. What counts is the spirit.'[19] When he was being as open and as expansive as this, you wondered how the myth of a difficult, silent, uncommunicative Beckett could possibly have evolved.

More fascinating and more fundamental still were some of the late-night conversations that were reported by the Dartmouth College professor, Lawrence Harvey, and the writer-translator, Patrick Bowles. He trusted both these friends and confided to them some of his most striking thoughts about the relations that he perceived between life and art. The great task for the artist,

Pierre Chabert in *Fin de partie*, 1999

Beckett said to Harvey, is to express 'being'. But 'being', he argued, is formless, chaotic, enigmatic and mysterious, 'a collection of meaningless movements'; man himself is inadequate, suffering, and disordered. Even though he is part of that meaninglessness, the artist is constrained to speak of it and in a language that will itself therefore be necessarily inadequate. Art, he went on, had commonly been thought of as a sign of strength and had never exploited that dark, chaotic area that constitutes 'being'. Seeking to explore what he called 'the authentic weakness of being', he commented to Harvey that 'whatever is said is so far from the experience' and 'if you really get down to the disaster, the slightest eloquence becomes unbearable'. To express 'being' more truthfully, he aimed at a breakdown of form, aspiring to what he termed a 'syntax of weakness'.[20] Some of the consequences of these views will be explored in the next essay.

Talks with Beckett did not always include such major insights into his attitudes towards life and art. But they were almost invariably of more than passing interest. During one dinner, for example, I remember that we had a conversation about schizophrenia, in which he talked of the nature and seriousness of Joyce's daughter Lucia's illness and of his doubts as to how definable such a condition really was. He confessed that he had not read R. D. Laing's book, *The Divided Self*, in which I suggested similar radical doubts were cogently expressed. The conversation then moved on naturally to the time when he himself had written about mentally ill patients in his 1938 novel, *Murphy*. It was then that he provided me with the interesting *aperçu* that he had actually *seen* his fictional character, Mr Endon (against whom Murphy plays a highly unusual game of chess), at the Bethlem Royal Hospital while visiting his psychiatrist friend, Geoffrey Thompson, who worked as a doctor there in 1934–5.

Over the years, I remember a number of discussions – informal 'chats' would be a more appropriate term – on philosophical questions with Beckett. Meeting for dinner once at the Hyde Park Hotel, where he often stayed when directing his plays in London, for example, Beckett asked me what I was

(Right) Robert O'Mahoney and Johnny Murphy in *Ohio Impromptu*, 1999

currently teaching at the university. As it happened, that day I had been conducting a seminar on the theatre of Jean-Paul Sartre. So I talked about Sartre's philosophy, arguing that, from my own perspective, we were too firmly *en situation* (too limited by our situation) for the existentialist's emphasis on human freedom to have a lot of meaning. Beckett agreed enthusiastically with this objection, saying that he found the actual limitations on man's freedom of action (his genes, his upbringing, his social circumstances) far more compelling than the theoretical freedom on which Sartre had laid so much stress. On several occasions he spoke of his great love for the writing of Schopenhauer, whom he read as early as 1930, and told me (in 1983) that he was currently reading an interesting essay by Karl Jaspers on that philosopher. We also once spoke of Pythagoras and of the Pythagorean theory of numbers, with Beckett playing down his knowledge of Greek philosophy and contrasting it with Joyce's great erudition. Yet notes that he wrote in the mid-1930s on Windelband's *History of Philosophy* have come to light since his death, showing how fascinated he was in man's various attempts to explain the universe and how much he did know about Pythagorean thinking.[21] So when he commented that he could detect 'no trace of system anywhere', his remark was made with a detailed knowledge of the many philosophical explanations that had been proposed over the centuries.

A third common myth was that Beckett was a total *miserabilist* and a pessimist, in his life as in his work. It is one of the most prevalent of misconceptions and is based, I believe, on a lack of knowledge of the complexity of the man, as well as on a profound misunderstanding of his work. There were certainly times when he could be sombre, intense and introspective: at such times, he would raise his hand to his furrowed brow, utter a weary sigh or go into a period of unbroken silence. All these reactions were familiar enough to anyone who spent any length of time with him. Friends had their own ways of coping with such crises: one would propose a game of chess; another used to talk about Dr Johnson to lift his spirits or play recordings of Mozart, Schubert, Haydn, Chopin, Beethoven or Webern;[22] another would wait patiently for the thaw to set in and for humour to reassert itself; yet another would babble away inconsequentially (myself, as it happens) hoping to interest him eventually in something that was being said.

In countering one myth, however, we should be wary of replacing it with another that is equally untrue. Self-evidently, Beckett was no Pollyanna. His despondency and gloom could be genuine and deep. Pain, suffering and distress impinged on him with extraordinarily sharp intensity and some of his most searing writing sprang from that keen awareness of pain and despair. There were times when he took lithium, prescribed to help him when he was at his most seriously depressed. He contemplated the future bleakly at times, even, it has been reported, to the point of occasionally contemplating suicide.

On the other hand, one can scarcely overstress the fierce personal resilience that he displayed when facing up to pain and adversity in his own life or, in general, the strength of his resolve to go on. Ultimately, suicide was unacceptable to him. A mixture of his Protestant upbringing and a stoic acceptance of life as a pensum that had to be endured as bravely as possible characterised his outlook. While researching Beckett's life, I was constantly surprised by his physical courage and his mental determination. In Germany in 1936–7, for instance, he operated himself on a blind boil on his hand with a razor blade. And, single-mindedly, he pursued his intellectual goals by visiting art galleries in Berlin, even though he had an excruciating lump under his scrotum ('between wind and water', as he put it).[23] Under such circumstances, most people would have caught the next train or plane home. But for Beckett that would have been running away and he never ran away. Indeed, he ran back to France from Ireland at the outbreak of the Second World War. Then, after returning to Ireland to see his mother once hostilities were over, he worked his way back there by taking a job with the Irish Red Cross Hospital in Saint-Lô.

This kind of resilience and strength of will characterised his entire approach to life and contradicts the negativity of which he has so often been accused. I remember writing to him shortly after Saul Bellow had won the Nobel Prize for Literature. At the end of the letter, somewhat misguidedly, I wrote: 'Another Nobel prize-winning pessimist'. Beckett wrote back wryly asking: 'Where did you get the idea I was a pessimist?'[24] In another letter to

Tom Bishop, he wrote: 'If pessimism is a judgement to the effect that ill outweighs good, then I can't be taxed with same, having no desire or competence to judge. I simply happen to have come across more of the one than of the other.'[25]

For, in both Beckett's work and in his life, there was a positive determination to persist, to go on regardless in what might appear to be the worst of straits. At the age of 75, he copied out these words of Edgar from *King Lear*: 'Who ist can say I am at the worst?'; 'The worst is not, as long as we can say, this is the worst.'[26] *Worstward Ho* became the title of the next spare, yet rich prose text that he wrote. There are also indications in his correspondence that he found the work of writers such as Thomas Hardy or T. F. Powys, in whom he identified an almost exclusively dark world-view, deeply rebarbative.[27] In his own work, even some of his blackest, bleakest sentences possess a shape, energy and dynamism that serve to negate nihilism.[28]

Beckett the man could be excellent company, often brilliantly witty. It was difficult to be with him for more than a few moments without laughter joining you as a third guest at the dinner table. I never failed to be surprised at how the lines around the eyes of this 'Aztec eagle' of a face, which appeared to have been etched deeply by pain and suffering, making him appear rather formidable, fell so naturally into laugh lines.[29] Few photographs reveal this transformation, for having his photograph taken was no laughing matter for Samuel Beckett. He tolerated it for the sake of his friends or as a minimal concession to publicity for the sake of the theatre or the production. The photos of him in this book, for instance, were all taken by John Haynes in a matter of moments at the Royal Court Theatre in London. Occasionally, he would agree to pose in his study for a photographer like Henri Cartier-Bresson, Lutfi Özkök or Gisèle Freund. But, even on his own territory, he disliked the self-exposure involved and looks tense and ill at ease in most of the photos.

His letters too are full of wry or genuinely witty remarks. When, on Suzanne's recommendation, he was being treated by a homeopath for cataracts on both of his eyes, he wrote sceptically: 'Still doing treatment for eyes. Silly drops, suppositories and homeopathic pellets, like a poultice on a

Samuel Beckett, 1973

wooden leg.'[30] 'Up to the cataracts in work',[31] he wrote or, since he had to wear dental plates following an operation for a cyst in his mouth, 'fed up to the plates with theatre'.[32] Here are a few of my personal favourites. It has been, he wrote, 'the worst Spring in the memory of daffodils',[33] a variant on 'no gardener has died within the memory of roses' from Diderot's *Le Rêve de d'Alembert*, over which he had chuckled as a young man, recycling the quotation several times in his early fiction.[34] When he found himself unable to write, he had, he wrote to a friend, 'nothing in [his] head but false teeth';[35] and, finally, speaking as an old man about his own health, he was 'on an even keel in the crooked last straight, there's metaphors for you'.[36] He always had the capacity to transform the cliché wittily, or to borrow another writer's *bons mots* and give them an unusual, idiosyncratic twist.

Even in old age, humour was an automatic reflex response to adversity. This very Irish trait was a constant lifeline for Beckett. It did not mean that he took harsh blows lightly. Humour is not always escapist. It can leave you still stranded, floundering in the eye of the storm, but it can also help to resist its buffeting by a kind of battening-down of the hatches. The things that Beckett laughed at were often the very issues that were gnawing away most painfully inside him: above all, ill health, physical degeneration and the failure to write. For years he joked openly about his 'bloody old bladder' and the state of his mouth, his

prostate, his eyes and his heart. But, in private, he worried obsessively as to whether the cyst growing in the roof of his mouth would in the end prove to be cancerous, whether the enlargement of the prostate from which he had suffered for years would also turn out to be malignant, whether, as his sight dimmed, he would, like James Joyce, slowly go blind and whether the frantically racing heart that had troubled him ever since his student days would finally lead to a heart attack, from which his father had died.

Two other apparently self-contradictory myths have been associated with Samuel Beckett. Because he could appear so distant, even absent, he was sometimes considered to be arrogant, even vain. Others spoke of him, however, as almost unbelievably modest, warm, generous and compassionate, almost a saintly figure, concerned with others to the point of softness and vulnerability. The truth (as so often with the human character) is infinitely more complex than either of these two extremes suggest.

As a young man, Beckett was remarkably clever, but intensely self-absorbed. This particular combination encouraged him to think of himself as superior to the majority of his contemporaries at Trinity College, Dublin. Reading his letters to friends, his early poems, his 1931 study of Proust, and his posthumously published novel, *Dream of Fair to Middling Women*, all written by the time he was 26, reveals indeed an outstandingly brilliant mind. Yet his feelings of superiority, isolation and apathy soon led him to experience what he himself described as 'terrifying physical symptoms': feelings of panic; a racing (or, as he termed it at the time, 'bubbling') heart; even, in its most acute manifestation, actual physical paralysis. Since a doctor friend could find nothing physically wrong with him, he came over to London from Dublin for a lengthy course of psychotherapy at the Tavistock Clinic under the care of W. R. Bion. After many sessions with Bion, in a letter to a confidant, Tom MacGreevy, Beckett produced a remarkably lucid, if cruel, piece of confessional self-analysis clearly based on the discoveries made with his psychotherapist.

(*Left*) Alan Howard, Denis Quilley and Ben Kingsley in *Waiting for Godot*, 1997

For years I was unhappy, consciously and deliberately ever since I left school and went into T.C.D. [Trinity College, Dublin], so that I isolated myself more and more, undertook less and less and lent myself to a crescendo of disparagement of others and myself. But in all that there was nothing that struck me as morbid. The misery and solitude and apathy and the sneers were the elements of an index of superiority and guaranteed the feeling of arrogant 'otherness', which seemed as right and natural and as little morbid as the ways in which it was not so much expressed as implied and reserved and kept available for a possible utterance in the future. It was not until that way of living, or rather negation of living, developed such terrifying physical symptoms that it could no longer be pursued, that I became aware of anything morbid in myself. In short, if the heart had not put the fear of death into me I would be still boozing and sneering and lounging around and feeling that I was too good for anything else.[37]

The diagnosis could not have been clearer: his physical problems were largely the product of feelings of superiority and isolation from others that were derived from a morbidly obsessive narcissism. We do not know precisely what Bion recommended. Yet, given the clarity of the diagnosis, the paths towards self-help and gradual cure were obvious enough: Beckett needed to counter his self-absorption by focusing his attention less on his own problems and by taking a much greater interest in and concern for other people. A basis for this already existed in the

Patrick Magee and Stephen Rea in *Endgame*, 1976

(*Left*) Conor Lovett in *Act Without Words I*, 1999

genuine kindness and love that he felt for his family and a few really close friends. The aim was to build on these positive foundations.

Initially, then, this shift in attitude probably occurred for purely pragmatic, therapeutic reasons. Yet the evidence of his friends suggests that what may once have been merely a search for a tolerable *modus vivendi* evolved into a more natural sharing in the problems, pain and suffering of others. In Beckett's case, it seems likely that Bion also encouraged him to externalise some of the obsessional or conflicting impulses within his psyche – his brooding self-analysis and attraction to quietistic apathy, for example, or his feelings of frustration and repressed violence – and direct them fruitfully into his writing. The experience of prolonged psychotherapy with Bion was probably one of the most fundamental factors in bringing Beckett to a radical reappraisal of himself and of his relationships with others.

Later events in his life, however, played a crucial part in his evolution from arrogant narcissist to caring philanthropist. In January 1938 he was stabbed close to the heart by a '*mec du milieu*' (a pimp) on a Paris street. Fears were expressed for his life. Had the wound been an inch to one side, his novel, *Murphy*, would have been published by Routledge later that year as 'by the late Samuel Beckett'. There would have been no *Waiting for Godot*; no *Molloy*; no *Endgame*. Beckett learned from the doctors at the Hôpital Broussais how dangerous his brush with the Grim Reaper had been and he never forgot. Such a near death experience can dramatically alter one's approach to life.

Then, in September 1941, as an Irishman resident in France, he joined a Resistance cell of the British Special Operations Executive in Paris: 'you simply couldn't stand by with your arms folded', he told Alec Reid.[38] His cell, 'Gloria SMH', was betrayed a year later by a Catholic priest and Beckett and his future wife escaped with only a few hours to spare, spending several weeks on the run, hiding in safe houses and little hotels, sleeping in barns, yards and ditches, tramping the roads, and fearing arrest at any moment. Many of his friends in the cell had been arrested and were he knew not where. Beckett and Suzanne lived out the remainder of the war in the little village of Roussillon in the Vaucluse until, towards the end of the conflict, Beckett once

again joined a local Resistance group. He returned to Paris through a war-ravaged France. All of these events shook him profoundly.

In another decisive experience, the months after the war that he spent working with the Irish Red Cross hospital in Saint-Lô in 1945 meant that he saw real suffering at first-hand. It was there that he witnessed devastation, destruction and misery: buildings, each of them someone's home, reduced to rubble by the bombing and the shelling; personal possessions blown to smithereens; a hospital, created out of nothing on fields that were a sea of mud; a ward full of patients ill with tuberculosis; people in urgent need of food and clothing, yet clinging desperately to life. One of Beckett's medical colleagues in the hospital, Dr Jim Gaffney, in letters home to his sister, spoke significantly not about Beckett's quiet, introspective manner, his sullenness or his moods of despair, but of his positive helpfulness, general kindness and thoughtfulness towards others.[39] Working as an interpreter as well as the storekeeper of the hospital, Beckett was forced to step outside himself to help those who were self-evidently much less fortunate than he. If he did not communicate with people, nothing got done.

His war experiences and the earlier lessons of psychotherapy seem, then, to have combined to distance him from the arrogant, self-obsessed young man he had been in the early 1930s. Even in the immediate post-war years, when they had little

Ben Kingsley and Alan Howard in *Waiting for Godot*, 1997

money, actively encouraged by Suzanne, who was herself spontaneously generous and had a keen social conscience, he helped out friends who were in worse need. Once *Waiting for Godot* started to bring in substantial royalties from the box office and from book sales in many countries, his kindness and generosity became legendary. Many individuals benefited directly from his financial help. Unannounced cheques would arrive in the post for hard-up friends, mostly without them asking. He did not even have to know the person to be willing to help. And the help was not only financial. A (once quite famous) French stage designer was having a very difficult time: 'could you possibly find him a job on one of your next productions?', Beckett asked one of his director friends. A writer friend had no income whatsoever: 'can you help to get him a travel grant to Poland?', he asked his Polish translator. An actor friend was out of work and his wife and children were living on food stamps in the United States: 'I'm trying hard to write a play for him', was Beckett's heartfelt response. Everyone seems to have had an example of his kindness and generosity. He was not a saint, but it is easy to see why some people thought of him in that way.

The older Beckett was painfully vulnerable. It was almost as if he felt the need to do extended penance for his youthful selfishness, arrogance and lack of concern. 'Never forget', one of Beckett's friends, the painter Avigdor Arikha, told me, 'that Sam had a tremendous sense of guilt.' This was very true. He blamed himself when he had no need and he did all that he could to allay his feelings of remorse by trying to make amends for the difficulties that life inflicted on those he knew. Even when walking in the street, he could never pass a beggar without giving him or her money. 'I know some of them are tricksters', he once said to me. 'But I can't take the risk.' The last phrase is massively revealing.

His responses almost always seem to have been motivated by spontaneous feelings of sympathy for the underdog: the failure, the invalid, the prisoner (political or otherwise), the beggar, the tramp or even the rogue. After the war in particular he seems to have had an almost total inability to filter out pain and distress, no matter who was experiencing it, combined with an exceptional capacity for listening and empathising.

But his ready sympathy and evident vulnerability laid him wide open to exploitation. He was notorious for being a soft touch. As a result, his friends tried to protect him from his own generosity. He often seemed like an innocent, unaware that he was being exploited or even, very occasionally, well and truly conned. There is one sense in which he was indeed an innocent. He always inclined to believe the best of someone, unless and until events proved the contrary. And because of his own loyalty and integrity, few people let him down. When one or two did, he was upset and mostly (though not always) forgave them for their (to use Winnie's phrase from *Happy Days*) 'human weakness . . . natural weakness'.[40]

Sometimes he knew perfectly well that he was being manipulated or even duped. His attitude was complicated by the fact that he rather liked rogues. One of the reasons for this was that he found their company a lot more fun than that of dour, respectable citizens, who quickly bored him. He had, after all, run away from respectable, middle-class, Protestant Foxrock, first to the less genteel, but more relaxed, convivial atmosphere of the Dublin bars, then to Paris, where the cult of *laissez-aller* prevailed, in artistic milieux at least, where your sexual preferences and conduct were a matter of more or less total indifference, and where no one worried if you drank too heavily. So a number of likeable rogues figured with the needy and the indigent among his acquaintances. And he

Barry McGovern in *Happy Days*, 1999

even derived a certain amount of wry amusement from being 'done' (as he put it) but not 'done in the eye'.[41]

Friends of Beckett have often spoken about his remarkable modesty as well as his incredible generosity as an older man. He was certainly self-deprecating, chiefly because he was so intensely self-critical. His unwillingness ever to be fully satisfied with what he wrote meant that he never became complacent, self-satisfied or lazy as a writer. He had learned from experience that cleverness and self-absorption could have disastrous personal consequences. And, like any really intelligent person, after the first flush of youthful arrogance, he had learned how much he did *not* know. Stupidity had become indeed not just a fact of life for him but a key element in an aesthetic of poverty, weakness and failure, in which he saw man as essentially a 'non-knower', a 'non-canner'.

I think to call him modest, however, is an oversimplification. In spite of feeling that words inevitably failed, he knew perfectly well what a superb stylist he was and how compelling his stage images were. He was also well aware of the literary and theatrical following that his work had attracted throughout the world and, although he disliked overt adulation, he did nothing to discourage the admiration and respect that he accepted as his due. Occasionally, in his later years, the sharp, irascible, younger Beckett would surface. Though normally very courteous, polite and tolerant, he could at times be difficult, curt and dismissive. Sometimes it was impatience with a tardy waiter; sometimes it was annoyance with an actress who failed to get his text right. I remember when he was discussing with me the heavy pressure that was being put on him by a particular producer who wanted him to compromise, he asked with pride as well as irritation: 'After all why should I have to work with the tenth-rate?' Yet the question seemed to me at the time (and still does) a good one: why indeed should he?

Any extended conversation with Beckett in the final years of the 1970s and early 1980s, as well as a review of his wartime record of involvement in the

(*Right*) Niall Buggy in *That Time*, 1999

Resistance (which remained unknown for so long because he kept it a secret, even from his closest friends), would have contradicted another prevalent myth that had arisen about him, namely that he took no interest at all in political events. This view is simply false. In conversation, he often discussed political oppression and the lack of freedom in the eastern European states, which had been under Stalinist domination since the end of the Second World War. He had a special interest in and affection for Poland, although he never visited the country. This may have been because his good friend, Henri Hayden, had been born in Warsaw and lived there until the age of 24. Beckett had also been in contact with a number of Polish editors, translators and directors since the mid-1950s and was on particularly friendly terms with Adam Tarn, the editor of the literary review *Dialog*. Tarn, who left Poland for Canada in 1968, published many of Beckett's plays for the first time in Polish in his review. Beckett had also met the well-known Polish playwright, Sławomir Mrożek, the author of *Tango*, on a few occasions in France and Germany, although they never became close friends.

At the beginning of the 1980s Beckett followed with deepening concern the dramatic events in Poland surrounding the rise of Solidarity, the demonstrations taking place in the shipyard of Gdansk and on the streets of other towns, then the subsequent arrests and the clamp-down that culminated in the Proclamation of Martial Law at the end of 1981. He had been corresponding for some years with a new Polish translator, Antoni Libera, who sent him hair-raising accounts of what was happening there to some of his friends. Libera himself was involved in the Defence of Workers movement, whilst his fiancée, Elżbieta, acted as an English language interpreter with Solidarity.

Beckett's immediate response to these reports was to arrange to have his Polish royalties paid directly to Libera for distribution to the families of arrested demonstrators or dissidents. He also paid for food parcels to be sent to the Liberas. At Beckett's request, I myself set up a bank account in England funded by him and, operating through the Polish Consulate and the British

(*Left*) Phelim Drew and John Olohan in *Rough For Theatre I*, 1999

Home Office, invited Libera to give some lectures. A similar plan was set in motion in the United States. The invitations were not at all innocent. We were in no doubt that the idea was, in Beckett's words, 'to get Libera out'. It was hoped that, once in the West, he might then apply for political asylum. The plan failed because Libera was refused his passport, for reasons said, ludicrously, to be 'a military secret'! He was then offered a passport, but only at a time when his fiancée's was withheld.

Anyone from the Eastern Bloc countries who managed to get out was welcomed and virtually guaranteed Beckett's wholehearted support, both moral and financial. He even once loaded piles of books from his own library into a taxi for a young Polish émigrée who was starting to do a doctoral degree on his work. Later on, he paid for his Hungarian translator to study in England.

One of the key misunderstandings concerning Beckett had to do with his position on political and humanitarian issues. It is often forgotten that he held an Irish passport right up to the end of his life and lived in France on a renewable, hence readily revocable, *carte de séjour* (or residence permit). His foreign status imposed certain restrictions on him, therefore, as far as joining in political demonstrations, signing manifestos, and so on. As a result, after the war his political activism operated mainly at a private and individual level.

Johnny Murphy and Ali White in *Catastrophe*, 1999

(*Left*) Phelim Drew, John Olohan and Robert O'Mahoney in *Rough for Theatre II*, 1999

Nonetheless, he still signed an appeal against the Proclamation of Martial Law in Poland at the end of 1981. In 1982 he dedicated a play, *Catastrophe*, to the Czech dissident writer Václav Havel. It has sometimes been suggested that this dedication was provided almost as an afterthought. In fact, it was written as a specific act of solidarity with Havel, who had been placed under house arrest, and the political dimension of the play, although by no means its only one, is vital to its significance. Its composition reflected Beckett's firm and constant opposition to all forms of totalitarianism – of the left or the right.

He told me that in the late 1930s, Suzanne, with whom he was then living although they were not married for another twenty years, had many Communist friends whom he also knew. He himself rejected Marxism as a system, yet his attitudes remained left-wing and anti-establishment. He was deeply and instinctively anti-racist. This explained the dangerous role that he played in the Resistance during the war, since he joined in the struggle against Nazism partly because of what was being done to his Jewish friends. In the 1970s he decreed that his plays could only be performed in apartheid South Africa provided that the audience was a multi-racial one. Effectively this meant that they could scarcely ever be played in that country. He also supported human rights movements such as Amnesty International and was a regular contributor to welfare organisations such as Oxfam and Save the Children. He was diametrically opposed to capital punishment and his horror at executions dates back to his first story, 'Dante and the Lobster', in *More Pricks than Kicks* (1934). His heart went out to all prisoners, whose treatment he considered as equivalent to the cruel caging of animals. He hated to hear the wailing and the clamouring of prisoners in the cells of the nearby Santé prison. All his moral and political attitudes revealed an intensely humanitarian concern.

Since the two-year period that he spent as *lecteur d'anglais* at the Ecole Normale Supérieure in Paris in 1928–30, when he met James Joyce and became a good friend of Thomas MacGreevy, who was attempting to carve out a career for himself as a poet and critic, Beckett was determined to write. His dedication to this aim was total and to ignore this aspect of his life in even the briefest of portraits would be unpardonable.

His father's death in 1933 meant that he inherited a small but regular income of £300 a year. But, in the 1930s and 1940s, in order to earn money he translated poetry and prose from French, Italian and, later, Spanish. From time to time he thought that he would simply have to get a regular job in order to make ends meet. He thought of becoming an assistant curator in an art gallery, for instance, and at one time even considered returning to university teaching, even though he had disliked it intensely when he had lectured at Trinity College, Dublin, and had quit his post after only a year and a half. Then, at the end of the war, with a large rise in the cost of living in France and the depreciation in the money coming from Ireland, his regular stipend proved insufficient for both him and Suzanne to live on. So for a while at least he found himself forced to give English classes and undertake translations for UNESCO and translate or supervise others' translations for Georges Duthuit's art magazine, *Transition*. All this time he felt compelled to write. Why he should feel such an urgent need to express remained a mystery to him. But it was one of his deepest certainties.

In fact, he achieved no real success as a writer until he was in his mid-forties. Before the war, the sales of his essay, *Proust* (1931), and his short stories, *More Pricks than Kicks* (1934), were fairly abysmal. His poems appeared first in literary magazines, then only in a small private press edition entitled *Echo's Bones and Other Precipitates* (1935). His novel, *Murphy*, which he finished in the summer of 1936, was turned down by over forty publishers and took two years before it came out. Even then it did not sell at all well. To persist up to that point must have demanded great strength of will and remarkable self-belief. But before he achieved success in post-war France with his novel trilogy, *Molloy*, *Malone meurt* and *L'Innommable*, and throughout the world with *En attendant Godot*, he recreated himself in several different ways.

First, he began to write in French. The enormity of this shift is often not fully appreciated. It is one thing to speak, write letters and conduct one's daily life in a foreign language, but quite a different matter, when one is not a native speaker, to create poetry, fiction or drama in a new language. Comparatively few writers have managed this feat successfully. One thinks, of course, of Conrad, Nabokov, and Ionesco. But examples are thin on the ground. Beckett studied French and Italian at Trinity College and, after graduating, he taught himself German, with some help from his younger cousin, Morris Sinclair. Studying several different languages helped him to achieve a greater objectivity and a more critical attitude with respect to his mother tongue. In a letter to Axel Kaun written in German in 1937, he wrote 'It is indeed becoming more and more difficult, even senseless, for me to write an official English.'[42] And so, a year later, he experimented with writing a number of poems in French that were simpler, more direct, less extravagantly erudite than the earlier English poems of the previous decade (with one exception, 'Cascando', written in 1936). He did not do this out of a desire for greater clarity. Indeed, in a 1938 review of Denis Devlin's poems he wrote: 'The time is not altogether too green for the vile suggestion that art has nothing to do with clarity, does not dabble in the clear and does not make clear.'[43] He hoped, rather, to attain an art in which, referring to Gertrude Stein, the 'texture of language has become porous'. 'More and more', he wrote to Axel Kaun, 'my own language appears to me like a veil that must be torn apart in order to get at the things (or the Nothingness) behind it.'[44] For his aim, as his conversations with Lawrence Harvey referred to earlier reveal, was to get closer to the expression of 'being' and of 'the mess'. He wanted, as he put it to Tom Driver, 'to find a form that accommodates the mess, that is the task of the artist now'.[45] A language that resonated with multiple associations and of which the writer appeared to be in control stood solidly in the way of these aims.

After his experiences during the war, when he had used French every single day of his life, it became easier for Beckett to write in that language. French allowed him, he claimed, to write 'without style'. He probably meant by this that it allowed him to use a language that was plainer, 'flowered' less exuberantly, and in which one could concentrate more on shape, rhythm and music. But he also undoubtedly meant a language that would offer fewer distractions from his own search for the 'essentials' of being.[46]

Secondly, soon after the war he had a 'revelation' in his mother's room in Foxrock, that has always been regarded as a pivotal moment in his writing career. Beckett himself presented it as a Saul on the Road to Damascus experience. In referring to it, he tended to define it as the point at which he recognised his own stupidity ('Molloy and the others came to me', he said, 'the day I became aware of my own folly. Only then did I begin to write the things I feel') and at which he realised that his true concerns lay in impotence and ignorance.[47] He reformulated this for me, for example, while attempting to define his debt to Joyce and to distinguish himself from his older friend and mentor. 'I realised that Joyce had gone as far as one could in the direction of knowing more, [being] in control of one's material. He was always adding to it; you only have to look at his proofs to see that. I realised that my own way was in impoverishment, in lack of knowledge and in taking away, in subtracting rather than in adding.'[48] Another element of significance to his own future work that emerged from the experience in his mother's room was the realisation that he should draw on his own inner world for his subjects: outside reality would henceforth be refracted through the filter of his own imagination; inner desires and needs would be allowed a much greater freedom; contradictions would be allowed in; and the imagination would be allowed to create alternative worlds to those of conventional reality.

Why he rejected the Joycean principle of knowing more as a way of creatively understanding the world and controlling it was because the world appeared to him as far more chaotic and less subject to control, man as much less rational and the self as much less coherent than such an approach implied. The consequences were that he turned his back on techniques that flowed directly from this principle, no longer incorporating, for instance, quotations and learned allusions into his work to build up an intellectually complex pattern of ideas and images. In future he resolved, he told me, that his work should focus on failure, poverty, exile and loss.

He repeated this version of his experience after the war many times, mostly in private conversations. Yet, in focusing on his so-called 'revelation' as a radical turning point – 'turning-point that was a great word with you', the voice of the Protagonist intones self-critically in That Time – Beckett introduced yet another myth into those that surrounded his life and career.[49] His subject matter certainly did undergo a significant change after the Second World War in the direction he described. His post-war writing in French was undoubtedly grounded more in feeling and in *not* knowing than in knowing. I am not suggesting that Beckett did not have a flash of insight akin to that described in the 'vision' that Krapp experiences in *Krapp's Last Tape*. What I am suggesting is that the revelation to which he drew attention was not a single Road to Damascus experience but rather a long drawn-out process, and that to see Beckett's work as divided into two parts, pre- and post-revelation, can easily distort our view of his development as a writer. As a number of critics have shown, some of his late themes were already deeply embedded in his earlier work, for example, the interest that he showed in Democritus' idea that 'nothing is more real than nothing' or the quietistic impulse that is present already in *Dream of Fair to Middling Women*. But the notion of a capitalised 'REVELATION' also hides several earlier, less sudden or less dramatic revelations: the certainty that he had to dissociate himself at an early stage from Joyce's influence; the reassessment of himself necessitated by almost two years of psychotherapy; the effect on him of being stabbed and in danger of dying; the freedom to discover himself as a writer that living away from Ireland freed from his mother's sternly critical influence offered him; the impact of the war years, when his friends were arrested and he was forced to escape and live in hiding; and the greater objectivity that working with others at St-Lô allowed him to assume with respect to his own inner self. The ground had been thoroughly prepared.

I also suggest that a recognition of ignorance was already to be found at the heart of his attitudes before the war and that, in spite of what he said, he never suppressed his own fierce attachment to learning. Beckett was, as his close friend Barbara Bray once put it to me, like a swan, sailing serenely along, spotting and picking up morsels from different parts of the lake, then predigesting them, before making them unequivocally his own. Commenting once on his formidable knowledge of Dante – with his pocket

(Right) Samuel Beckett, 1973

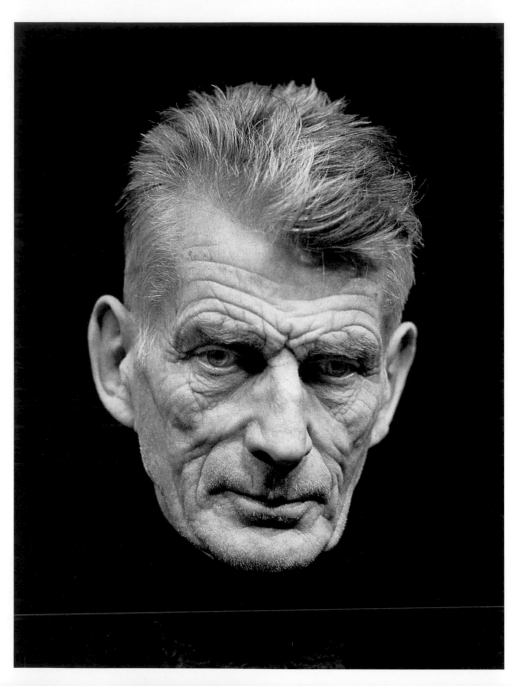

student edition of Dante lying on the table in front of us at the time – I made the, to me at least, obvious remark that he was something of an expert on the great Italian author. 'No, I'm not an expert', he said decisively. 'To be an expert on Dante, you'd have to know all the Latin works, and I don't know them all.' As a true scholar, he knew how little, relatively speaking, he did know. In an entry in his German diary, dated 15 January 1937, he revealed how his swan-like instincts stemmed from a coherent theory of knowledge, and, conversely, of ignorance:

> I am not interested in a 'unification' of the historical chaos any more than I am in the 'clarification' of the individual chaos, and still less in the anthropomorphisation of the inhuman necessities that provoke the chaos. What I want is the straws, flotsam, etc., names, dates, births and deaths, *because that is all I can know* . . . [italics mine]. I want the old-fashioned history book of reference, not the fashionable *monde romancé* that explains copiously why e.g. Luther was inevitable without telling me anything about Luther, where he went next, what he lived on, what he died of, etc.[50]

My experience in working on Beckett's biography as well as on his drama convinces me that his links with learning and his debts to the past, as well as to the contemporary artistic world, along with experiences culled from his inner and outer life, have, in many instances, simply gone underground in his later work. In other instances, they have become so closely integrated into the

Samuel Beckett, 1973

fabric of the work that they are no longer apparent. They survive there, however, like bacteria in the lower intestine, healthy and active within the body of the text. The ways in which learning was used merely evolved in his later writing, as his acceptance of the inner as well as the outer chaos found expression in poetic, and, in the later plays, pictorial or sculptural form.

Beckett always saw himself – his post-war, as well as his pre-war self – as part of a continuum with the European literary and artistic past. We cannot, therefore, understand the remarkable leaps of the imagination that he made to produce some of the most radical work in prose, drama and television of the twentieth century without knowing where he is leaping from or the factors that provoked the stunning acrobatics that he performed with word and image.

Images of Beckett

Writing to a friend, the American director, Alan Schneider, in 1972 about his new (and, at that stage, still unperformed) play, *Not I*, Samuel Beckett described the spotlit image of Mouth, suspended high in the darkness, as 'purely a stage entity, part of a stage image and purveyor of stage text. The rest is Ibsen.'[1] His comments established a clear, if elliptically expressed, distinction between his own approach to the theatre and the more traditional plot-based, character-based drama epitomised by the great Norwegian dramatist. Taken along with Beckett's other letters concerning his plays to Schneider and his theatrical notebooks, however, they also direct attention to the importance that he accorded to his stage images. As a director of his own plays, he would often concentrate, as he put it, on the 'picture', working to get the stage image as close as possible to what he had in mind.[2] At the Royal Court Theatre in London in 1976, I watched him adjusting May's posture in *Footfalls* for a full half-hour before he was satisfied that he had finally got it right. He also spent a long time checking with the set and costume designer Jocelyn Herbert and the actress Billie Whitelaw that May's costume was insubstantial enough to echo the 'tangle of tatters' referred to in the text.[3]

The powerful imagery of his stage and television plays makes a good case for considering Beckett as an important visual artist, who influenced artists with very different styles, from the minimalist painters Geneviève Asse and Robert Ryman, to Avigdor Arikha, Edward Gorey, Dellas Henke, Louis le Brocquy and Jasper Johns, as well as film, video and installation artists like Bruce Nauman, Stan Douglas, Valie Export, Tony Oursler, Rodney Graham, Steve McQueen and Ugo Rondinone, among many others.[4] The art critic, Werner Spies, asked the rhetorical question, 'Where are the fundamental texts that might serve as *legenda aurea* for painting, object art, Actionism or video installations?' and answered: 'Here we encounter first and foremost Beckett.' In drawing parallels between Beckett's work for the theatre and television and Bruce Nauman's early video work, Spies goes on to suggest that 'in general, much of what minimalism offers is grounded in Beckett's visual abstinence'.[5]

(*Left*) Billie Whitelaw in *Not I*, 1973

'Visual abstinence' is rather a good term for Beckett's late theatre, since he often employed only a single or a double image, illuminated in the surrounding dark, empty spaces: Mouth in *Not I*, with the figure of a shrouded Auditor, standing upright, a surrogate spectator, on the other side of the stage; an old man's head with hair outspread, looked at 'as if seen from above', in *That Time*; a woman in a rocking-chair, rocking herself into death in *Rockaby*; a male figure clad in a nightgown standing by an oil-lamp in *A Piece of Monologue*; a woman pacing to and fro in *Footfalls*, 'revolving it all in her poor mind'; a Listener with long white hair seated at a table with another figure, Reader, 'as alike in appearance as possible', in *Ohio Impromptu*. The earlier plays, *Krapp's Last Tape* and *Happy Days*, are in turn an unusual monologue and a two-hander, referred to originally by Beckett as a 'Female Solo', in which Winnie's companion, Willie, often invisible to the audience, utters only a few brief words.[6] *Play* has the relative profusion of three heads but, immured in funeral urns as they are, they cannot move. Again, there are three figures – entire bodies this time rather than fragments – in *Come and Go* and in *Catastrophe*, but in the latter play written for Havel with one of them, the Protagonist, standing almost entirely motionless. Beckett's first produced play, *Waiting for Godot*, has the extravagance of having four

Billie Whitelaw in *Footfalls*, 1976

(*Right*) Alan Howard and Alex Russell in *Waiting for Godot*, 1997

characters, plus a boy messenger sent from Mr Godot. Yet for much of the time Estragon and Vladimir appear as lonely figures, isolated in time and space. In *Endgame*, there are four players, but two of them are invisible for a large part of the play, incarcerated as they are in their ashbins, leaving Clov as the only one able to move around the stage, serving Hamm who sits in his wheelchair.

As his theatre develops, especially from *Happy Days* (1962) and *Play* (1964) onwards, the images that Beckett creates also become increasingly static, concentrated, and spectral. They hover somewhat precariously on the fringes of materiality; yet they remain exceptionally powerful, bold, even startling. However close to diminution, even dissolution and disappearance, they may be, they never fail to make a huge impact on the spectator, especially on someone seeing them for the first time.

There is little doubt that Beckett's focus on powerful stage images coincided with his fundamental mistrust of language, even if it did not necessarily derive from it. In all likelihood, this mistrust stemmed from his reading in the 1930s of a critique of language from the Nominalist German linguistic philosopher, Fritz Mauthner, *Beitrage zu einer Kritik der Sprache* (1901–2), as well as from his own increasingly sceptical position.[7] For, after the linguistic extravagance and erudition of his early poems, Beckett found that he could not celebrate the word in James Joyce's terms. Writing to Axel Kaun in 1937, he already foresaw in a letter quoted earlier what he described as 'a literature of the unword', writing:

> As we cannot eliminate language all at once, we should at least leave nothing undone that might contribute to its falling into disrepute. To bore one hole after another in it, until what lurks behind it – be it something or nothing – begins to seep through; I cannot imagine a higher goal for a writer today . . . Is there any reason why that terrible materiality of the word surface should not be capable of being dissolved, like for example the sound surface, torn by enormous pauses, of Beethoven's Seventh Symphony, so that through whole pages we can perceive nothing but a path of sounds suspended in giddy heights, linking unfathomable abysses of silence?[8]

(*Left*) Johnny Murphy and Ali White in *Catastrophe*, 1999

The cameraman at Süddeutscher Rundfunk, Jim Lewis, a good friend of Beckett's, recounted a conversation that he had with him in 1982, in the course of which Beckett said that every word he used seemed to him to constitute a lie and that music (in the sense of rhythm) and image were all that were left for him to create.[9] 'Words', he had told Lawrence Harvey in the 1960s, 'are a form of complacency'; writing was, he said, as if one were 'trying to build a snowman with dust'; nothing holds together.[10] But it is worth stressing again that his attempt to break down traditional forms of language stemmed from the wish to express 'being', which he saw as essentially formless, chaotic, enigmatic and mysterious.[11]

Beckett was probably drawn to the image initially for reasons similar to those of the English novelist and art historian, Anita Brookner, who said in a recent interview that 'Images have a striking power to crystallise certain moments, certain feelings: a sort of immanence.'[12] Beckett often spoke of how the image was more powerful than the word and superior to it in its greater clarity and precision. 'Thus the image of a knife is more accurate than the word knife . . . "knife" has no meaning, it's a blurred image. You have to say "butcher's knife", "kitchen knife" "a knife to cut the bread" so that the word takes some meaning. But when it is shown, you see at once what kind of knife it is: the image is then stronger than the word.'[13] Beckett often used images in a direct, strong, confrontational manner. In its most extreme form, if an ejaculation was the closest one could get to pure being, as Beckett suggested to Harvey it was, the scream and the image of the open mouth waiting to 'scream again' in Not I comes closer to expressing one aspect of 'being' than any of the formal structures of language could do.[14]

But Beckett's thinking on the image went beyond the attractions of crystallisation and immanence. The actor, Stephen Rea, tells a revealing story of how, while he was rehearsing the part of Clov in Endgame, he asked Beckett a question: 'Clov keeps repeating to Hamm: "I'll leave you, I'll leave you." I pointed to one particular instance of this and said to Beckett, "When he says it at this point, does that mean he is going to the kitchen or is he going for

(Left) Patrick Magee and Stephen Rea in Endgame, 1976

good?" Beckett replied "It's always ambiguous."[15] Beckett's stage images, too, possess an ambiguity that is essential to conveying some of the mysteries of being. No explanation is offered as to why Estragon and Vladimir should be keeping their appointment with Mr Godot. Similarly, why Nagg and Nell live in dustbins or why Winnie is buried in a dying earth and is exposed to the searing heat of a cruel sun is never explained. Mouth's predicament in *Not I*, Listener's situation in *That Time* and May's in *Footfalls* are simply 'as stated', a disembodied mouth and a head compelled to utter, a woman compelled to pace. The image exercises its own powerful impact on the spectator or the viewer, puzzling as well as overwhelming.

Images virtually usurp the position of words in some of Beckett's late television plays: *Quad* uses hooded figures moving across a square to the rhythm of percussion beats; *Nacht und Träume* uses a seated figure of the Dreamer and introduces the pictorial elements of a visitation, with the words of Schubert's *Lied* being sung. In *Ghost Trio*, language is still present in the play, but less prominent and less powerful in its effects than the almost abstract shapes, the slow movements of the Protagonist, and the music of the Largo of Beethoven's 'Ghost Trio'. Three different, interrelated images hold the attention in *. . . but the clouds . . .*, even though the resonant words of W. B. Yeats' poem 'The Tower' still supply a moving verbal element to the play. However, although visual images seem to dominate or even to supplant words in the late plays, the importance of their role in his earlier dramas should not be underestimated. They intrigued, moved and impressed and were what so many spectators remembered.

The first question that we might legitimately ask is what the main sources of Beckett's dazzling array of images could have been. Did they spring fully fledged from his creative imagination? Or were they extensions, transformations or distortions of images that he had encountered in real life? Even with the figure of Winnie in *Happy Days*, buried first up to her waist, then her neck in the ground, the latter suggestion is not as preposterous as might at first appear to be the case. One has only to think of someone being

(*Left*) Rosaleen Linehan in *Happy Days*, 1999

covered with sand (for fun) on a holiday beach or, in a more sinister vein, of the torture employed by the Foreign Legion when a miscreant was exposed to the remorseless heat of the sun by being buried in the desert, to realise that the boldness of the imaginative leap came simply from believing that an entire play could be created out of such a stark situation. The figure of the Auditor in Not I derived, Beckett himself acknowledged, from an everyday situation when he was on holiday in Morocco, as he watched a djellaba-clad woman standing motionless and rigid, waiting, it emerged later, for her child to arrive. A number of autobiographical explanations have been put forward to account for the presence of many other images and elements in Beckett's plays: the turnips, radishes and carrots with which Estragon and Vladimir are preoccupied, for example, in Waiting for Godot were rare treats to Beckett and Suzanne in real life as they tramped south to the Vaucluse during the war, after the betrayal of their Resistance cell to the Gestapo; similarly, a pair of boots that might fit or a night's rest on the hay in a barn that the two friends in Godot long for must have seemed at the time like luxuries.

Hamm in his wheelchair in Endgame has been seen to echo the situation of Beckett's aunt, Cissie Sinclair, whom he used to wheel around when she was crippled with arthritis, and who used to ask him to 'straighten up the statue'. Beatrice Lady Glenavy wrote that Endgame 'was full of allusions to things in her [Cissie's] life, even the old telescope which Tom Casement had given me and I had passed on to her to amuse herself with by watching ships in Dublin Bay or sea-birds feeding on the sands when the tide was out'.[16] And I have suggested in my biography of Beckett that Endgame almost certainly drew on Beckett's recent experiences of the sickroom, as his brother lay dying, particularly the way in which time slowed down to a painful crawl, as they waited for an ending that they knew was imminent but would, seemingly, not come.[17]

Real-life situations, however, too often provide inadequate and unconvincing explanations of the sources of Beckett's stage images. Their origins are usually more mysterious and certainly more complex. For evidence has emerged recently that suggests that it was his artistic experiences that provided him with a rich, primary vein of inspiration to be tapped, for he

had a remarkable ability to draw on his knowledge of one artistic medium and see its possibilities for transformation and use in another.

Beckett himself pointed us in this particular direction. One day, when he was standing in the Nationalgalerie in Berlin with a friend, the theatre scholar, Ruby Cohn, in front of Caspar David Friedrich's painting, *Mann und Frau den Mond betrachtend* (*Man and Woman Observing the Moon*) he commented memorably: 'You know that is the source of *Waiting for Godot*.' The painting he had in mind was, in fact, the very similar *Zwei Männer betrachten den Mond* (*Two Men Observing the Moon*) from Dresden's Gemäldegalerie, which he had seen during an artistic pilgrimage to Germany in 1937. Friedrich's painting lay behind the way in which, when he directed the play himself at the Schiller Theatre in Berlin, Beckett imagined the scene at the end of both acts in which the two tramps, standing by a skeletal tree, were silhouetted against the moonlit sky. He even wrote the artist's name 'K. D. Friedrich' on a page of his directorial notebook, which faced his analysis of the moonlight scene.[18] He did not attempt – at that point in the play, at least – to copy the actual postures of the two observers in the Friedrich painting, in which both figures were painted from the back looking together at the moon, one with his arm placed affectionately around his companion's shoulder. Instead, first Vladimir and then Estragon turned separately to contemplate the

Ben Kingsley and Alan Howard in *Waiting for Godot*, 1997

risen moon. Yet Beckett clearly aimed to recreate something of the atmosphere of the German Romantic painter's celebrated canvas. Even the tones of the set and the costumes in Beckett's production seem to have reflected the coloration of the original painting, with its carefully modulated greys, browns and black.

Beckett also wrote to me in April 1973 about his play, *Not I*, in which Mouth pours out a stream of sound with a huge figure of a standing, listening Auditor: 'image of *Not I* in part suggested by Caravaggio's *Beheading of St John the Baptist*'.[19] This huge, powerful painting hangs in the oratory of St John's Cathedral in Valletta, Malta, where Beckett and Suzanne spent a holiday in 1971, just before he started to write *Not I*. The crucial elements for Beckett's play are the head of John itself, reduced further by Beckett to the bold image of a babbling mouth, and the observing spectators – most movingly, an old woman with her hands held over her ears, which, when it coalesced with the memory of the Moroccan waiting figure, became the Auditor, capable only of making gestures 'of helpless compassion'.[20] Since Beckett had already had the idea of a head spouting out words like water from a fountain many years before, the importance of Caravaggio's painting was to provide an insight into the way in which the two different images might be configured in practice on stage.[21]

In the light of these known examples (and a mass of new evidence gleaned from personal correspondence and from private diaries that Beckett wrote while he was in Germany in 1936–7) the question then poses itself: do unrecognised artistic sources of inspiration lie behind some of his other theatrical images?[22] It would indeed be surprising if, when Beckett came to create his own images for the stage, traces of his knowledge of paintings should not have survived and, sometimes consciously (as with *Waiting for Godot* and *Not I*), sometimes quite unconsciously, have exercised an impact on both the genesis and the form of his own startling visual theatrical imagery. Like a man who consumes large quantities of garlic, often unknown to himself, his breath, even the pores of his skin, emits its powerful odours.

(*Left*) Caspar David Friedrich, *Two Men Observing the Moon*

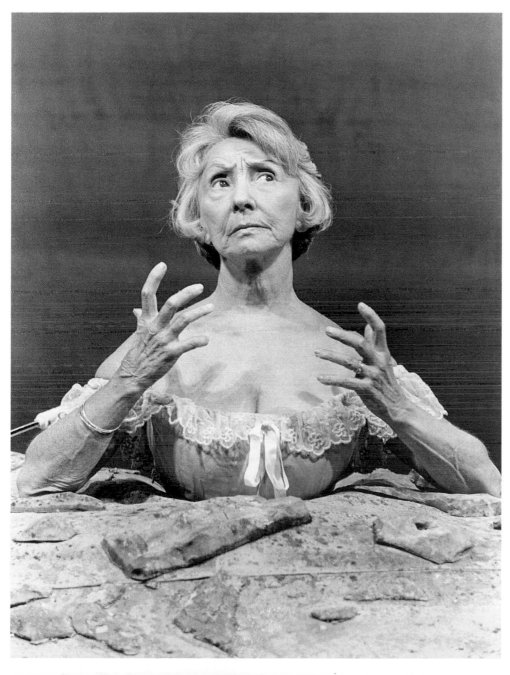

This claim does not, I think, diminish Beckett's stature as a writer and a visual artist; quite the contrary. It fits him into the artistic as well as the literary continuum in which, as we saw at the end of the first essay, he placed himself – a bold, radical innovator who, nonetheless, owed a huge debt to the past.

After the Second World War, Beckett wrote several published pieces of trenchant art criticism. *Three Dialogues with Georges Duthuit* consisted of a remarkable series of exchanges about modern art that he had with the art critic Georges Duthuit, the son-in-law of Henri Matisse. He also wrote essays on the Dutch painter brothers, Bram and Geer van Velde, as well as shorter pieces on the Polish-born French painter Henri Hayden, the Irish painter and writer Jack B. Yeats, and the Israeli artist Avigdor Arikha, all of whom were among his personal friends.[23] These publications and friendships suggest that Beckett's interest in art centred almost exclusively on modern painting. In fact, his main love throughout his life remained the work of the Old Masters, as Arikha confirmed to me. That the impact of their paintings on his work has been ignored is not only because of an earlier lack of evidence, but precisely because Beckett's theatrical imagery appeared so startlingly radical and innovative and because his approach to the world seemed to derive from a post-existentialist, post-Expressionist consciousness. He was indeed

Madeleine Renaud in *Oh les beaux jours*, 1969

(*Left*) Caravaggio, *The Beheading of St John the Baptist*

acutely aware of developments in modern art and his own imagery was, as we shall see later, profoundly modified by this knowledge. But one of his most significant contributions to the theatre was to have drawn visual inspiration from the work of the Old Masters, and yet to have created theatrical images that take on a distinctively modern form, and, in some cases, even assume iconic status, as the image of the two tramps waiting for Godot certainly has done. A look at Beckett's personal relations with painting may help to explain how this convergence of ancient and modern came about and to judge how important it was for his own writing for the stage.

Ever since his youth, Beckett had an astounding, perhaps even a photographic, visual memory for subject, form and colour in painting. Although the central character, Murphy, in Beckett's 1938 novel of that name, has great difficulty in calling to mind the faces of his own mother and father, he has a very vivid recollection of a face in a painting that Beckett saw in the National Gallery in London just before he wrote the novel: 'He saw the upturned face of the Child in a Giovanni Bellini Circumcision, waiting to feel the knife.'[24] Even in his early eighties, Beckett could himself remember very clearly details of Old Master paintings that he had seen many years, even decades, before. As a young man, for example, visiting the National Gallery of Ireland in Dublin, he had seen Salomon van Ruisdael's landscape painting depicting a coach halted at a coaching inn, entitled *The Halt*. Some sixty years later, Beckett could still describe to me the tiny, almost indistinguishable, figure of a boy urinating against a wall.[25] In fact, he sometimes called this painting not *The Halt* but *The Urinator*.[26] According to Arikha, he could spend as long as an hour in front of a single painting, surveying it, savouring its forms and its colours, reading it, absorbing it in its most intricate details.[27] Often it was the tiny narrative or human aspects that he could remember and pick out in a seventeenth-century Dutch canvas.

The extent of his passion for painting, its intensity and the range and depth of his knowledge of the Old Masters, has gone largely unrecognised until very recently – except by a handful of close friends and a very few critics. His almost encyclopedic knowledge of art was well known, for example, to

his friend and later director of the National Gallery of Ireland, Thomas MacGreevy, with whom Beckett corresponded at length in the 1930s, frequently about painting. But their correspondence has not been readily available and, as I write, it can be read only on microfilm in Trinity College, Dublin. Over the years, Beckett sent literally hundreds of reproductions, mostly of Old Master paintings, to his friends, from postcards to poster-size reproductions, and in turn received them back; as a priority, he visited art galleries and churches that held important paintings, in whichever large town or city he found himself, both before and after the Second World War; he bought dozens of catalogues of art collections, many of which still exist today, handed on by Beckett to Arikha; and he acquired numerous books on painting. As faithful as the most assiduous lover, he went back to see particular paintings that he admired, even adored, time after time after time. In the 1930s he swapped ideas on their attributions with MacGreevy, doubting sometimes what the curators and the official catalogues said about the artist. And he discussed specific details of paintings: a hand, a foot, a colour, the state of preservation of a canvas, or the restoration work that had been done or that needed doing. He had an excellent eye. The line of the left leg of a figure in a Giorgione painting is wrong, he suggested to MacGreevy – and the experts concluded that the leg had indeed been painted over in the nineteenth century.[28]

Beckett's ability to draw parallels and to make fascinating comparisons was astounding. In 1937 he compared, for instance, the shepherd in a Signorelli painting in the Kaiser Wilhelm Friedrich Museum in Berlin with an El Greco that he had last seen in London two years before.[29] His confidence in his own aesthetic judgement was (to me at least) breathtaking. His best and most realistic idea for gainful employment in the 1930s, when writing was bringing him in almost no income at all, was to apply for the post of assistant curator at London's National Gallery.

We can discern a number of important stages in Beckett's artistic Odyssey. He seems to have fallen in love with painting first while he was a student at Trinity College, Dublin, in the early 1920s, although his interest may already have been nurtured by his aunt, Cissie Sinclair, who was herself a talented painter – mainly of portraits and still lifes. Cissie trained at the Dublin Metropolitan School of Art under Sir William Orpen with Dorothy Elvery, who herself painted Beckett when he was a child, and Estella Solomons, a friend of Beckett's uncle, William 'Boss' Sinclair.[30] With his brother, Harry, William Sinclair worked as an art dealer, first in Dublin, then in Germany.

Beckett visited the National Gallery of Ireland regularly, first as an undergraduate, then as a lecturer in Trinity College in 1930–1. He was weaned on the gallery's eclectic collection of Old Masters. It was in Dublin, not in London, Paris or Berlin, for example, that he first developed an abiding passion for seventeenth-century Dutch painting. He loved Dublin's van Goyen, *A View of Rhenen on the Rhine*, and was so familiar with other van Goyens in European galleries that, later on, he would refer in letters or private diaries to an actual physical landscape as 'very van Goyen'. He found the National Gallery's Rembrandts splendid: the *Portrait of a Lady Holding a Glove* (now thought to be from the studio of Rembrandt, although still catalogued in 1981 as by Rembrandt), the astounding *Rest on the Flight into Egypt* and, from an imitator of Rembrandt, *Portrait of an Old Gentleman*. These were the first of many paintings that Beckett saw by an artist with whom he developed a highly ambiguous relationship, lost at times in admiration for Rembrandt's uncompromising artistry, yet turning away from his darkness and his gloom.

It was in the National Gallery of Ireland, too, that Beckett first encountered a member of the Brueghel family, the son, Pieter Brueghel II, 'Hell Brueghel' as he is known, in the form of *The Peasant Wedding*. The likely impact of Brueghel the Elder's paintings on Beckett's stage imagery will be discussed later. *The Entombment* by Nicholas Poussin, whose paintings Beckett always admired, stunned him with its lyrical colours of blue and purple, and Cuyp's *Milking Cows* and Titian's *Ecce Homo* impressed the young Beckett so much that they became interesting points of reference or comparison for him during his wider safaris into the European galleries. The paintings of Adriaen Brouwer, of which Dublin had one example, *The Corn Doctor*,[31] always excited his interest and he used to call the artist 'Brouwer, dear Brouwer'.[32]

A second and important stage of Beckett's artistic apprenticeship was in Kassel in Germany at the end of the 1920s, when he used to visit his uncle, 'Boss' Sinclair, and his wife, Cissie, who had moved to Kassel from Howth in Ireland some years before. Beckett often went to Germany, because he was having a somewhat turbulent love affair with their daughter, his cousin, Peggy.[33] Her father, William Sinclair, was associated at the time with a small circle of practising painters, art collectors and connoisseurs, for, as well as teaching English, 'the Boss' worked at that time as a part-time art dealer in Kassel. It was there that Beckett came into his closest contact so far with modern art. This happened not so much in the city art gallery, where he undoubtedly went to look at the Old Masters, but on the Sinclairs' walls and in 'Boss' Sinclair's own collection of modern German art, some of which was stored for him at the museum. In the last year of his life, Beckett could remember seeing a fine Lyonel Feininger painting, entitled *The Bathers*, hanging over the Ibach piano in his aunt's flat. His uncle also owned a Boccioni, entitled *Laughter*, and a fine painting by Heinrich Campendonk, probably one called *Die Einsame* (*The Lonely One*).[34] For Beckett, these were crucial, highly formative encounters with modern works of art.

Beckett also saw hanging on 'Boss' Sinclair's wall Ewald Dülberg's *Abendmahl* (*Last Supper*) that we now know only from a photograph. The canvas itself has not yet been traced. Dülberg was a personal friend of William Sinclair and a regular caller at their apartment. It was Dülberg's painting with Christ's Apostles depicted as bald eggheads that Beckett evoked in his early poem, *Casket of Pralinen for the Daughter of a Dissipated Mandarin*, and even explicitly described in his novel, *Dream of Fair to Middling Women*:

> He [Belacqua] goggled like a fool at the shrieking paullo-post-Expression of the Last Supper hanging on the wall fornenst him, livid in the restless yellow light, its thirteen flattened flagrant egg-heads gathered round the tempter and his sop and the traitor and his bourse. The tempter and the traitor and the Jugendbund of eleven. John the Divine was the green egg at the head of the board. What a charming undershot purity of expression to be sure! He would ask for a toad to eat in a minute.[35]

Ewald Dülberg, *Last Supper*

Dülberg painted in Expressionist mode and, of the moderns, Beckett was especially drawn to the work of the artists of the *Brücke* group and the *Blaue Reiter*.

There followed a two-year period in London in 1934–5, when Beckett was in England for a course of psychotherapy with W. R. Bion at the Tavistock Clinic. He became a regular visitor to the city's main public art galleries, especially the National Gallery, the Victoria and Albert Museum and the Wallace Collection.[36] At this time some of the great paintings of the English and Irish national galleries became like old friends to Beckett. It was during this period (as we shall see in a moment) that he thought most deeply about art and absorbed the iconography of the Old Masters so thoroughly that he could draw on it at will.

This was followed by a vital six-month-long visit to the German art galleries in 1936–7, when, through contacts that he made in Hamburg, Berlin, Dresden and Munich, he managed to view some important private collections as well as those of the major public galleries. He also visited some of the less famous art collections in Brunswick, Halle, Leipzig and Erfurt and wrote regular accounts of his reactions to individual paintings in hundreds of pages of personal diaries, which contain some of his most precisely formulated aesthetic judgments. These diaries continue to bear witness to his enormous admiration for Old Masters such as Giorgione, Caravaggio, Rembrandt, Antonello da Messina, van Honthorst, van Goyen and Wouwerman. But they also reveal how keen he was at the time on the work of Expressionist painters such as Emil Nolde, Franz Marc, Ernst Ludwig Kirchner (a personal favourite of Beckett), Lyonel Feininger, Karl Schmidt-Rottluff and Erich Heckel.

Hardly surprisingly, in view of this passionate interest in art, Beckett's early essays, poems and prose reveal many allusions to painting, often subtly fused with literary allusions or elements taken from real life: in the poems, 'Sanies I' (Botticelli), 'Sanies II' (Puvis de Chavannes), 'Serena III' (Hogarth), 'Malacoda' (van Huysum); in *More Pricks than Kicks* (Cranach – a hidden reference – Dürer, Paul Henry, Hogarth, Masaccio, Perugino, Pisanello,

Rodin, Uccello, Andrea del Sarto and Velazquez); in *Murphy* (Avercamp, Bellini, Parmigianino, Rembrandt and Tintoretto); in *Watt* (Bosch, Jan de Heem); and in his correspondence with MacGreevy (the Master from Delft, Geertgen tot Sint Jans, Elsheimer, Fabritius, Hercules Seghers, the School of Patinir, Ruisdael, Cézanne, etc.). In 'Love and Lethe', one of the stories of the 1934 collection, *More Pricks than Kicks*, for instance, the figure of the Magdalene is proposed as a visual approximation to the 33- or 34-year-old Ruby Tough: 'Those who are in the least curious to know what she looked like at the time in which we have chosen to cull her we venture to refer to the Magdalene in the Perugino Pietà in the National Gallery of Dublin, always bearing in mind that the hair of our heroine is black and not ginger.'[37] In 1931, only a few weeks before he left Dublin to resign his lectureship from Germany, Beckett had raced breathlessly round to the National Gallery of Ireland as soon as he heard that Perugino's newly purchased *Pietà* was on display. And, in a letter to MacGreevy, written only after he had seen the picture several times, he wrote: 'The Christ and the women are lovely. A clean-shaven potent Xist [Christ] and a passion of tears for the waste. The most mystical constituent is the ointment pot that was probably added by Raffaela . . . a lovely cheery Xist full of sperm, and the woman touching his thighs and mourning his secrets.'[38]

Paintings were not uncommonly invoked in his early prose to evoke the mood expressed by a face, by the eyes in particular, to which, as in his own life, Beckett was hyper-sensitive. The face of the woman in the Dublin pub selling seats in heaven in his story 'Ding-Dong' ('tuppence a piece . . . four fer a tanner') is compared, for example, with the face in the National Gallery by the Master of Tired Eyes that, like other tormented faces Belacqua had seen, 'seemed to have come a long way and subtend an infinitely narrow angle of affliction, as eyes focus on a star'.[39]

Most striking of all, perhaps, by way of a parallel is the evocation of the changes that take place in the Alba's eyes in Beckett's first novel, *Dream of Fair to Middling Women*, written in 1932 but published only posthumously: 'Her great eyes went black as sloes, they went as big and black as El Greco painted, with a couple of good wet slaps from his laden brush, in the Burial of the

Johnny Murphy, Alan Stanford and Barry McGovern in *Waiting for Godot*, 1999

Count of Orgaz the debauched eyes of his son or was it his mistress? It was a remarkable thing to see. Pupil and white swamped in the dark iris gone black as night.'[40] Seán O'Sullivan's portrait of his close friend, Ethna MacCarthy (on whom Beckett based so many aspects of the character of the Alba and whom he adored), shows her extraordinarily large, beautiful black eyes and more than justifies the seemingly oblique parallel with the El Greco painting in Toledo described here by the narrator.

The influence of the Old Masters went much deeper, however, than these passing allusions suggest. Beckett once said that Christianity was a 'mythology with which I am perfectly familiar so I naturally use it', and his plays display a close familiarity with the Christian imagery of painting.[41] *Waiting for Godot*, for example, was shaped almost as much by crucifixion imagery as it was by Caspar David Friedrich's moonlight painting. Entire sections of dialogue are concerned with the issue of damnation and salvation. When Beckett directed *Godot* at the Schiller Theatre in Berlin, he echoed on many occasions paintings of Christ between the two thieves. Pozzo, raised from the ground and slumped between the two tramps, almost mirrors pictures of the Descent from the Cross, or even, at times, a ludicrous *Pietà*.[42] Pozzo and Lucky fell on the ground forming a cruciform pattern, and when

Vladimir did the Tree, although he was adopting a position in yoga, he was also restating in oblique, passing form that same crucifixion theme.

The evidence of Beckett's fascination with crucifixion imagery is also displayed in his draft play manuscript fragments, as well as in his correspondence and in doodles discovered in his private notebooks. In 1937 he wrote to Tom MacGreevy about a number of paintings in the illustrated catalogue of Munich's Alte Pinakotek: 'I was very interested also in the stiff-legged Cranach Crucifixions and the Burg[k]mair ditto, with the thieves in less than profile. An idea for a Christ crucified with his back to the spectator.'[43] In fact, he tried to write just such a play in the early 1950s, in which the central image was that of a man elevated on a cross, although not with his back to the spectator.[44]

In *Endgame*, a blood-stained handkerchief covers Hamm's head at the beginning and end of the play, calling to mind the legend of Saint Veronica, whose napkin was said to have retained the imprint of Christ's face. Beckett had already alluded to this image in an early poem, 'Enueg II': 'veronica mundi / veronica munda / give us a wipe for the love of Jesus'.[45] Golgotha, the 'place of the skull' (Matthew 27:33) and the crucifixion itself are evoked obliquely many times in Beckett's writing: in Lucky's 'think' ('the skull, the skull') and in the images of the charnel house and of bone and stone in *Waiting for Godot*. The skull-like set of *Endgame* picks up visually a theme that is stated as Hamm directly associates himself with Christ, partly by his question 'Can there be misery . . . loftier than mine?', which surely echoes George Herbert's poem 'The Sacrifice', in which Christ calls out as a refrain: 'Was ever grief like mine?'[46] The names, too, in *Endgame* (Hamm, Clov, Nagg, Nell) are all variants of hammer and nails. For Beckett, nails invariably recalled the Crucifixion.[47]

Several of the late plays evoke religious imagery subtly, in ways that considerably deepen the resonance of the text. In *Catastrophe*, a play written for Václav Havel when he was under house arrest, the director's attempt to reify the protagonist can be viewed as an attempt to reduce a living human

(*Left*) Alan Stanford and Barry McGovern in *Endgame*, 1999

being to the status of icon of impotent suffering. His flesh is whitened to approximate stone or white marble; his hands are forcibly raised to his chest like the praying stone-like figures in a Mantegna painting or the representations found on marble monuments. Behind this powerful image, suggested obliquely, lie centuries of an iconography of a crucified Christ or of martyred saints: van Honthorst's arrow-pierced body of Saint Sebastian, for instance, from the National Gallery in London, or Antonello's 'magnificent' (the word was used by Beckett in his German diaries) painting of the same saint from the Gemäldegalerie in Dresden.[48] In the end, the tormented victim in Beckett's play will not accept stasis, martyrdom or defeat and raises his head in a single act of silent but resolute defiance.

In his television play, *Nacht und Träume*, Beckett introduced a number of elements that were borrowed almost literally from religious art. In religious paintings, a vision often appears in the top corner of the canvas, normally the Virgin Mary, Christ ascended in his glory, or either one angel or a band of ministering angels. In Beckett's television play, the hand coming from above the Dreamer bearing a cup suggests the chalice, and the cloth that appears to wipe his brow evokes once again the Saint Veronica handkerchief;[49] the hand placed on that of the Dreamer is the hand of comfort and solace, reminding us that for years Beckett had a reproduction of Dürer's praying

Johnny Murphy in *Catastrophe*, 1999

hands on the wall of his room in the family home.[50] It has also recently been suggested that *Nacht und Träume* recalls paintings of the Agony in the Garden by Bellini, Mantegna, a copyist of Correggio and Gossaert.[51]

The presence of Christian imagery (both visual and verbal) in Beckett's plays does not, of course, make him a Christian or even a religious dramatist. Often such images offer a hope of salvation that is never realised. Often, too, man is presented as a victim, trapped in his own suffering in a hostile world with an absent, indifferent, if not actively malevolent deity. Yet such religious images leave behind traces of spiritual aspiration, if not transcendence. And, at the very least, these frequently hidden or half-hidden echoes of religious paintings (or writings) suggest far more than they state, weaving complex patterns of the explicit and the implicit. In Zeifman's words, 'it is this wedding of the implicit with the explicit that provides Beckett's drama with its extraordinary religious density, the wellspring of both its beauty and its power'.[52]

The positions, postures and gestures of some of Beckett's late protagonists recall obliquely figures in Beckett's beloved seventeenth-century Dutch paintings. They sit motionless or freeze their movements into immobility, moving steadily towards, yet still resisting, stasis. As visual parallels, one thinks particularly of late Rembrandts or late Vermeers – those now

Pierre Chabert and Henry Pillsbury in *Fin de partie*, 1999

oh so familiar figures seated on a chair or at a table: the *Old Man in an Armchair* attributed to Rembrandt or his authenticated *Portrait of Jacobsz Trip* from the National Gallery in London, whom it is hard to resist seeing as a pre-modernist Hamm in Beckett's *Endgame*.

In *Krapp's Last Tape*, Krapp, as he leans over his tapes or grips the microphone on the table, takes on a striking resemblance to Vermeer's *Geographer* in Frankfurt, who stands hunched over his charts, a set of dividers in one hand. In its pendant painting in the Louvre, *The Astronomer*, well known to Beckett from the late 1920s, could almost be a view of Krapp seen from the wings of the theatre, hand and book on table, right hand outstretched in Vermeer's painting towards the Hondius globe or, in Beckett's play, towards the Gründig tape recorder or ledger.

The setting – room, table and props – of *Krapp's Last Tape* may even have been partially inspired by an early painting of Rembrandt, *The Parable of the Rich Man* or *The Money Changer* (1627), that Beckett saw in the Kaiser Wilhelm Friedrich Museum in Berlin in 1937.[53] In this picture, the 'rich man' sits in a pool of light cast by a candle held in his left hand, holding up a gold coin in his right hand. He is surrounded by his account books bound in vellum, heaps of bills, promissory notes and a huge money-bag, all piled up on the table around him. When he wrote the play, Beckett did not have the benefit of Tümpel's 1971 elucidation[54] of this painting as related to Saint Luke's account of the rich man hoarding his gold in large barns in the hope of living a bountiful material life on his hoard, but being called to a prompt account by God: 'Thou fool, this night thy soul shall be required of thee: then whose shall those things be, which thou hast provided? So is he that layeth up treasure for himself, and is not rich toward God.'[55] But he was very familiar with the gospel text – so much so that he cited it in his 1966 television play, *Eh Joe*[56] – and was quite capable of making the link himself between this and the rich man's hoarding of his riches. Krapp's tapes have commonly been referred to as the modern equivalent of a writer's journals or diaries. Yet they can also be seen as attempts to store up accounts of his key experiences, like a miser hoarding his gold. And, in the same way as the man who lays by treasure in the Book of Luke, Krapp is himself waiting for the visit of the Grim

Reaper, discovering that what had once seemed most important to him now appears worthless and that what he had once rejected outright now seems important. With Krapp seated at his table in a pool of light with his register, his tapes, his dictionary and his tape recorder, focusing intently on his taped treasures, *Krapp's Last Tape* has, then, both visual and thematic affinities with the small Rembrandt painting in Berlin.

Beckett's later play, *Ohio Impromptu*, with its two almost still figures sitting with a hat lying on a plain white table, is a thoroughly Rembrandtesque composition, although Avigdor Arikha has surmised that Terborch's painting, *Four Spanish Monks*, in the National Gallery of Ireland may well have been a source of inspiration for this play.[57] The image of the woman rocking herself into death in *Rockaby* looks, on the other hand, like a fascinating fusion of ancient and modern. One thinks perhaps first of Rembrandt's *Margaretha Trip (de Geer)* that Beckett knew well from the National Gallery in London, and of the flashes of light and colour from the jet sequins on the dress of the woman in *Rockaby* that perhaps echo the magnificent Giorgione self-portrait that so captivated Beckett in Brunswick in 1937. Perhaps memories of *Whistler's Mother* in Whistler's painting or Madame Roulin in Vincent van Gogh's *La Berçeuse* are also evoked within the image. Certainly the closing moments of Beckett's play have something of the ambiguity of Jack Yeats'

Rembrandt, *Portrait of Jacobsz Trip*

painting, *Sleep*, in which an old woman sits by the window, her head drooping low onto her chest in sleep or in death.

The sceptic would, of course, say that any man or woman sitting in an armchair or standing at a table would look like Hamm, Krapp, the Reader or Listener, or W in *Rockaby*. But would they? And when we know that Beckett was steeped in the visual imagery of these paintings and that, over a period of years, he could compare different paintings by the same artist in some of their most intricate visual details, the parallels or echoes become at the very least highly intriguing.

But is the technique of what we might call 'imaginative blending', that is, borrowing and transforming many different elements from different areas of his experience into a new creation, one that came naturally to Beckett? It certainly did in his early days. Let us take one example by way of illustration from the stories, *More Pricks than Kicks*, and the novel, *Dream of Fair to Middling Women*, on which some of those stories were based. Here his methods were far more transparent. We see that he blended together (in a highly inventive, even extravagant fashion) elements in his prose that he had borrowed from real life, from literature and from art. For his description of the physique of one of his female characters – in his novel, *Dream of Fair to Middling Women*, she was the Smeraldina Rima and in the

Joan O'Hara in *Rockaby*, 1999

(*Left*) Albert Finney in *Krapp's Last Tape*, 1973

story 'Draff' she became Mrs Shuah – he borrowed and then caricatured a few features from a real-life person, that of his cousin, Peggy Sinclair, with whom he had had a love affair: her body 'mammose, slobbery-blubbery, bubbubbub, the real button-bursting Weib, ripe' was indeed in reality a little out of kilter with 'the sweetest little pale Pisanello of a bird-face ever',[58] although nothing like as grotesquely as this account might suggest. But, as John Pilling has demonstrated, Beckett also borrowed for his description of the Smeraldina entire quotations from Burton's *Anatomy of Melancholy* ('she was pale, pale as Plutus'; 'blithe and buxom and young and lusty'; 'the double-jug dugs', etc.), which he juxtaposed with quotations from Dante about Sordello ('Posta sola soletta' and 'tutta a se romita').[59] He also drew on his knowledge of painting: the Smeraldina/Mrs Shuah has 'Botticelli thighs' as well as the 'Pisanello of a bird-face' and, he wrote, varying his allusion only slightly in the two works, 'She was like Lucrezia del Fede, pale and belle, a pale belle Braut.'[60] This reference to the portrait of Lucrezia del Fede by Andrea del Sarto in the Prado in Madrid or another in the national gallery in Berlin is of particular interest, because it bears an uncanny resemblance to photographs of Peggy Sinclair that have been preserved.

Later in his career, Beckett became much less allusively dense, weaving both fewer literary quotations and fewer allusions to art into his plays and prose texts, although such echoes were not entirely lacking in his post-Second World War writing. The plays, as well as the novels, were, however, still heavily influenced by the visual arts. As we saw with autobiographical material, both literary reminiscences and artistic imagery were more fully absorbed, sinking deep beneath the surface, or were more successfully integrated into the creative process itself. One feels, nonetheless, that, if it were possible to take X-ray pictures of Beckett's stage images, they would reveal some of the ghost-like figures of the Old Masters that have inspired visual elements in his plays.

The impact of Beckett's great interest in art is even discernible in his directing of his own plays. Billie Whitelaw commented aptly that, when he directed her in *Footfalls*, 'he was not only using me to play the notes, but I almost felt that

he did have the paint-brush out and was painting'.[61] He was concerned to ensure that his bold, powerful, resonant images and 'frozen tableaux' should make their maximum impact in the theatre. One sure way of achieving this was to draw on his wide experience and deep knowledge of art and channel them into his practice as a director. For, in all his own productions, Beckett showed that he was as aware as any painter or sculptor of the many different visual elements involved in the staging or televising of his plays: the overall composition within the frame, whether of the proscenium arch or the television screen; the disposition of figures in space; the power, yet ambiguity of the visual images he had created; the source, intensity and quality of the light; and the choice of colours from a deliberately restricted palette.

Some of the most fleeting tableaux in Beckett's own Schiller Theatre production of *Godot* recreated, almost in passing, scenes from paintings by the Old Masters. We have already seen how much the moonlight scene owed to Kaspar David Friedrich. Two others in particular bring to mind pictures by Pieter Brueghel the Elder. One, *The Parable of the Blind*, was recreated in act 2 (with reduced numbers it is true) by Pozzo following his guide, Lucky, on a shorter lead; Pozzo resembled the figure in the painting who has fallen to the ground. Similarly, the scene in which all the characters fall over and lie with their legs

Greg Hicks in *Waiting for Godot*, 1997

outstretched, gazing up at the zenith, also bore a close resemblance to Brueghel's other painting, *The Land of Cocaigne*, that Beckett saw in Munich's Alte Pinakotek in 1937. Lucky's initial unforgettable appearance revealed a grotesque who could have existed quite happily and relatively unremarkably in the world of Bosch or Brueghel.

When Beckett directed Billie Whitelaw in the role of May in *Footfalls* at the Royal Court Theatre in London in 1976, her posture, as she paced to and fro across the stage, with her arms tightly folded across her body, was carefully shaped to echo that of the painting of the *Virgin of the Annunciation* by Antonello da Messina, which again Beckett had seen in Munich's Alte Pinakotek in 1937. Advising the director Donald McWhinnie on his production of *That Time*, which was on the same programme, he ensured that Patrick Magee's head, wearing a huge wig of long white hair fully outspread, bore a close resemblance to William Blake's paintings of God the Father or Job.

Many of these influences may not have been conscious at all. They probably stemmed from what could be termed 'memory traces', traces left behind by encounters with paintings that had affected Beckett deeply. For an iconography had been so totally absorbed by Beckett that his creative imagination could draw upon it as naturally and as unostentatiously as he did on the Scriptures, Dante or Milton, Racine or Leopardi, Shakespeare or Hölderlin. And, as with so many of his literary

Antonello da Messina, *The Virgin of the Annunciation*

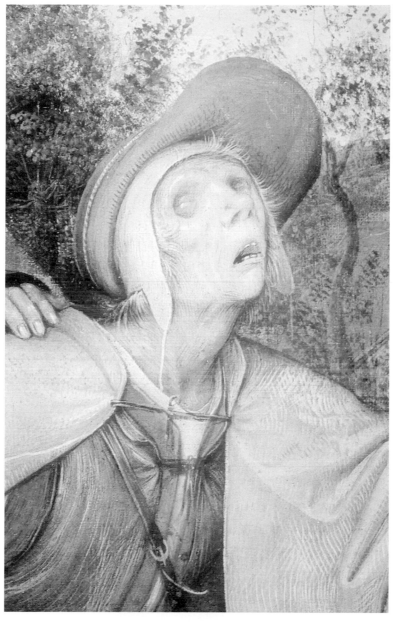

sources, his remarkably retentive memory meant that he had no need to 'revisit' a particular painting in order to draw on it for inspiration, shaping his own images in the light of earlier works of art, yet making them entirely his own.

As a student in the 1920s, Beckett regularly used to go with friends to plays at the Abbey Theatre in Dublin. According to one of them, he once remarked how much a principal actor, Michael Dolan's 'hands came into expressing his feelings' when he played the role of a modern Job in T. C. Murray's play, *Autumn Fire*.[62] Later, when lecturing on the plays of Molière at Trinity College, he stressed how essential the 'muscular dialogue generated by gesture', which Molière had himself inherited from the *commedia dell'arte* tradition, was to the success of seventeenth-century theatre.[63] But, above all, Beckett seems to have been fascinated by the expressive, frozen gestures seen in paintings: hands raised in prayer or outstretched in compassion; a finger raised in blessing or admonishment; a man holding an open book; a lady intent on what she is writing; a hand raised to the breast, chin or brow; a woman playing cards or making lace.

Beckett carried over some of the force of these gestures into his own theatre. Gestures in his plays are restrained rather than grandiloquent, but nonetheless they appear stark and powerful

Detail of grotesque figure in Pieter Brueghel the Elder, *The Parable of the Blind*

because they are few in number, are repeated as echoes of one another and are formally and meticulously organised. *Come and Go* is built, for example, upon the same patterns of repeated, rhythmic movements, as each of the three women goes off stage in turn while the others speak of her illness or imminent death; during her absence, a finger is raised to the lips of one of the remaining pair in an unspoken 'sshh'. This emphasis on the hands then culminates in the crossed hands of the three women, seated on the bench together. In *Ohio Impromptu* attention is focused on the 'bowed head propped on right hand' of both the Reader and the Listener, then on the left hand of the Listener knocking sharply on the table. In *Catastrophe* the Director's female assistant essays several different positions for the joined hands of the statuesque Protagonist, before finally raising them breast-high in a posture that echoed Dürer's picture of praying hands.[64] In *Nacht und Träume* the consoling hand, as we have seen, echoes visually the supernatural hand of comfort that appears in many religious paintings, with or without the chalice.

When he was directing his own plays, Beckett lavished immense care on the placing of the hands of his protagonist. Billie Whitelaw wrote of her work with him on *Footfalls*: 'Sometimes I felt as if he were a sculptor and I a piece of clay. At other times I might be a piece of marble that he needed to chip away at. He would endlessly move my arms

Patrick Magee in *That Time*, 1976

Conor Lovett in *Act Without Words II*, 1999

and my head in a certain way, to get closer to the precise image in his mind.'[65] In Beckett's German production of *Endgame*, Nagg and Nell's hands as they emerge from the ashbins were placed 'at a set distance apart and their symmetrical placement on the rims of the ashbins. There they rest unmoving save for when they have a task in the action, like Nagg's right hand in the biscuit episode.'[66] And in *Krapp's Last* Tape, the 69-year-old Krapp cupped his hand around the corner of the tape recorder, while his younger recorded voice said, 'I lay down across her with my face in her breasts and my hand on her.'[67] Beckett's fascination with gesture (which was a virtual obsession) almost certainly resulted from his deep immersion in the visual images of the Old Masters.

Beckett's use of lighting in his plays from the 1958 *Krapp's Last Tape* onwards may also owe something to 'spotlighting' as a technique in painting. As early as 1935 he revealed a special interest in the history and development of 'spotlight painting' as a genre. He wrote to Tom MacGreevy: 'It is very hard to see the Elsheimers in the German room [in the National Gallery in London] but the *Tobias & the Angel* seems exquisite . . . The Geertgen *Adoration* [the *Nativity* by Geertgen tot Sint Jans, also in the National Gallery] must be one of the earliest spotlight paintings. Surely it is only half the story to date them from Raphael's *Liberation of St Peter*. I never saw the Oxford Uccello mentioned in this

connection either.'[68] He had just been reading R. H. Wilenski's *An Introduction to Dutch Art* (1929) and taking notes on Wilenski's discussion of how Elsheimer used spotlighting to 'evoke a mood', but his final comment to MacGreevy on the 'Oxford Uccello', which was added to his notes on Wilenski, reveals that he was also thinking widely about the genre as a whole.[69]

Neither Rembrandt nor Caravaggio are considered to be spotlight painters as such. But both create striking chiaroscuro effects, contrasting light and darkness, isolating figures against a dark background. Of the dozens of paintings by Rembrandt that we know Beckett knew well, I think of his famous *Self-Portrait in Old Age* at the National Gallery in London, where virtually only the head is at all brightly lit, and his *An Elderly Man as St Paul*, also from the National Gallery. For actual spotlight effects, one tends to think of paintings such as *The Denial of St Peter* in Amsterdam or *The Adoration of the Shepherds* in London.

As for Caravaggio, we have already noted the impact that *The Beheading of St John the Baptist* from Valletta Cathedral in Malta had on Beckett. The head of Goliath in Caravaggio's *David with the Head of Goliath* from the Borghese Gallery in Rome is just as striking. The human head is frequently isolated in Caravaggio, as in the 1600 *Supper at Emmaus*, against varying dark brown tones. All of the heads are painted with heavy shadows created by the light that comes so often from the left. Some of these Caravaggio images reverberate in the mind, when one thinks of Beckett's own visual pictures in plays such as *Not I*, *That Time* and *Catastrophe*. They may well have been in Beckett's mind too, as we know one of them certainly was, and the heads that emerge out of the surrounding darkness in his plays appear to be genetically related to the images of Rembrandt and Caravaggio.

But a number of lesser-known, though still important, painters used lighting effects in ways that intrigued Beckett. One such painter whom he admired very much was Gerrit van Honthorst ('Gherardo delle Notti', as he was known in Rome). More important still are the 'exquisite' (Beckett's word

(*Left*) Ingrid Craigie, Ali White and Susan Fitzgerald in *Come and Go*, 1999

again) paintings of Adam Elsheimer, a sixteenth-century German painter who spent a long time living and painting in Rome.[70] Art critics have long debated whether Elsheimer was influenced in his 'night pieces' by Caravaggio or by the earlier work of Altdorfer, Bassano or Bellini. What is clear is that he was strikingly original in his treatment of light. Sometimes his beautiful night effects are achieved by creating scenes with bonfires, torchlight or moonlight, as in his *Flight into Egypt*, seen by Beckett in the Alte Pinakotek in Munich in 1937 (which has all three sources of light), or *St Paul on Malta* in London's National Gallery.

When Beckett started to work in a practical way in the theatre, he became fascinated by the effects of light and shade that stage lighting could produce: faces emerged starkly out of the darkness in *That Time*, *Rockaby* and *Catastrophe*; shadows fell on the ghostly figure of May in *Footfalls* and on Krapp in *Krapp's Last Tape*, in the latter case created first by the spotlights, then by the swinging lamp over Krapp's table. There were instances when the links seemed even more specific than this. Bearing in mind Beckett's lighting directions for *Footfalls* – 'Lighting: dim, strongest at floor level, less on body, least on head'[71] – it is interesting to note that Elsheimer lights his figures at times from the ground up (as in the *Mocking of Ceres*), the level of light diminishing as it plays on the faces of his human figures. When Beckett came to direct the play himself, he found that this device worked less well on stage than it did in a painting, and he felt obliged to add front-of-house lighting to illuminate the face when May halts to speak. And he made other changes that demonstrate the impact that art had had upon him.

In rethinking *Krapp's Last Tape* for the Berlin stage, for instance, he altered the visual appearance of his play by introducing a lit 'cagibi', a den or cubby-hole, situated at the back and to stage right. So, at the start of the play, instead of having everything laid out on the table in advance, as described in the original published texts, in the revised stage directions, after opening a black, opaque curtain that, at first, covered the entrance to this tiny annex to his room, Krapp went into his den to carry out, one by one, the objects that he needed to enact a birthday ritual of listening, and, later, of recording. Beckett's directorial notes reveal that, in the Schiller Theatre production,

the entrance to the white monk-like cell, into which Krapp disappeared periodically, was left open throughout the play, until the light there was faded with the rest of the stage lighting at the end. And so, crucially, the cubby-hole echoed the zone of light in which Krapp sat or stood, yet differed from it in size and shape. As Krapp went in to drink or to fetch a dictionary or a microphone, his shadow became clearly visible on the white wall of the den.

The addition itself is highly reminiscent of the paintings of the seventeenth-century Dutch artist Pieter de Hooch, who often painted a brightly lit background scene viewed through a doorway or an archway. This provided an inner frame within the main frame of the picture and supplied another light source. We may recall in particular the painting entitled *The Mother*, which Beckett saw in the Kaiser Wilhelm Friedrich Museum in Berlin on his trip to Germany in 1936 7.[72] This was also reproduced in black-and-white illustration in Wilenski's *Introduction to Dutch Art*.[73] Among the many other paintings of de Hooch that use this characteristic motif are *The Pantry* in the Rijksmuseum in Amsterdam, *The Card Players* in the Queen's Collection at Buckingham Palace, and a family group, *Woman with Child and Maid*, in the Kunsthistorisches Museum in Vienna. Beckett may not have been consciously inspired by any particular de Hooch painting, but the introduction

John Hurt in *Krapp's Last Tape*, 1999

of such a lit den was the natural choice of a visual artist steeped in seventeenth-century Dutch art.

Although some of Beckett's stage images were inspired by the Old Masters, they are much more deeply problematic, more desperate and more anguished than his sources of inspiration. In this respect, they bear the unmistakable stamp of modernity. The disparities between the different worlds are crucial. In the Caspar David Friedrich painting, for example, which Beckett quoted as the source of *Waiting for Godot*, the moon is used as a symbol of Christ and his promised return; consequently, for Friedrich, it was a symbol of hope.[74] In Beckett's play, the echo of *Two Men Observing the Moon* seems rather to be making an ironic comment on the protracted wait for a Godot, who in the end, of course, never comes. Antonello's virgin in the picture that I related earlier to *Footfalls* is calm and serene; Beckett's twisted, tormented figure, on the other hand, has hands that are hooked around her arms like claws and her mouth is agape in a silent scream. Mouth in *Not I* or May in *Footfalls* may in the end have more in common with Edvard Munch or Francis Bacon than with Caravaggio or Antonello. ('In *Footfalls*', wrote Billie Whitelaw, 'I sometimes felt like a walking, talking Edvard Munch painting.'[75])

Beckett's images were problematic primarily because they derived from a much more troubled view of the relationship between the artist and the world. In the modern world there was, Beckett wrote in an article on 'Recent Irish Poetry' in 1934, a 'rupture of the lines of communication' between subject and object.[76] It was his encounters in the mid-1930s with the paintings of Cézanne and with the highly innovative works that his Dublin friend Jack B. Yeats was painting at that time that gave him the opportunity to express most fully his views on the relations between the painter, his painting and the world.

Beckett saw Cézanne's landscapes as constituting a huge break with painting tradition, especially the anthropomorphic landscapes of the past. He wrote to Tom MacGreevy: 'Cézanne seems to have been the first to see

(*Left*) Pat Kinevane, Phelim Drew and John Olohan in *What Where*, 1999

landscape and state it as material of a strictly peculiar order, incommensurable with all human expressions whatsoever. Atomistic landscape with no velleities of vitalism, landscape with personality *à la rigueur*, but personality in its own terms, not in Pelman's *landscapality*.'[77] Then, choosing as his example a work by a painter that he liked, Jacob van Ruysdael's *The Entrance to the Forest* in the National Gallery in London, he went on to express a subtle yet clear perception of man as severed from an alien outside world:

> Ruysdael's *Entrance to the Forest* – there is no entrance anymore nor any commerce with the forest, its dimensions are its secret and it has no communications to make . . . So the problem . . . of how to state the emotion of Ruysdael in terms of post-impressionist painting must disappear as a problem as soon as it is realized that the Ruysdael emotion is no longer authentic and Cuyp's cows as irrelevant as Salomon's [van Ruisdael's] urinator in Merrion Square except as a contrivance to stress the discrepancy between that which cannot stay still for its phases and that which can . . . How far Cézanne had moved from the snapshot puerilities of Manet and Cie when he could understand the dynamic intrusion to be himself and so *landscape to be something by definition unapproachably alien, unintelligible arrangement of atoms*, not so much as ruffled by the kind attentions of the Reliability Joneses [italics mine].[78]

That Beckett loved and admired many of these anthropomorphic landscapes was largely irrelevant. He saw them as right for the time in which they were painted (a time when, as he put it, 'the animising mode was valid') but no longer right for modern man.[79] And, in defining what he saw as Cézanne's recognition that landscape had nothing to do with man, that man was quite separate from it and alien to it, he recognised that he was outlining an attitude that was, for him, excitingly close to his own view of the world as a 'no-man's land'.[80]

Looking at Yeats' painting next in a way that the painter himself would probably not have recognised as his own, Beckett went on to extend this alienation, isolation and solitude to human beings, who are irretrievably

(*Left*) Barry McGovern, Johnny Murphy, Stephen Brennan and Alan Stanford in *Waiting for Godot*, 1999

cut off not just from nature but also from each other. He wrote, again to MacGreevy:

> I find something terrifying for example in the way Yeats puts down a man's head and a woman's head side by side, or face to face, the awful acceptance of 2 entities that will never mingle. And do you remember the picture of a man sitting under a fuschia hedge, reading, with his back turned to the sea and the thunder clouds? One does not realize how still his pictures are till one looks at others, almost petrified, a sudden suspension of the performance, of the convention of sympathy and empathy, meeting and parting, joy and sorrow.[81]

Speaking many years later of his continued admiration for Yeats' work in a letter to Georges Duthuit,[82] Beckett admitted that when he talked about art, he was invariably expressing his own obsessions, his own bleak, uncompromising vision of human separateness and loneliness, a vision that was already present in his 1931 study of Proust, in which, pushing Proust's pessimism further than most readers would allow, he wrote elliptically: 'We are alone. We cannot know and we cannot be known.'[83]

It was to be over ten years before Beckett managed to accommodate this view of the artist and the world successfully in his own writing. When he did, it enabled him to draw inspiration for his stage images from the iconography of the Old Masters that he knew so well, but, at the same time, to express a vision that was startlingly modern and very much his own. Man in Beckett's world is cut off from the empty heavens and nature offers him distraction but no consolation: 'You and your landscapes!' says Estragon to Vladimir, adding 'Tell me about the worms!'[84] The tree is there only as a potential gibbet, from which they consider hanging themselves. Vladimir and Estragon need each other's presence, but each regularly finds himself isolated in his own solitude or suffering. When Estragon sleeps, Vladimir feels his loneliness; when Vladimir sings, Estragon becomes despondent. Others seem to cultivate their solitude: in *Endgame*, Clov cannot wait to escape from Hamm back into his kitchen and Nagg and Nell are confined to their ashbins, into which they have been discarded, like household rubbish. Winnie is incarcerated in a mound of earth from which she cannot escape and has minimal contact

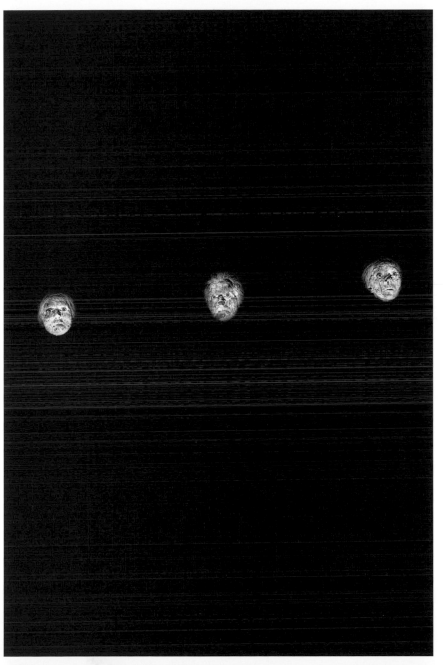

with her husband, Willie. The three figures in their urns in *Play* are totally separated from one another. Mouth in *Not I* relates the tale of a lonely, alienated life, while May in *Footfalls*, who 'has not been out since girlhood', paces up and down in the room of a deserted house.[85] Alienation of all kinds became a constant in Beckett's theatre: alienation from the world, alienation from the other; alienation from the self.

Whenever he had the opportunity, Beckett sought out the work of modern painters, and, in the late thirties in particular, he became friendly with many painters, not only the Dutch van Velde brothers, Geer and Bram, about whom he wrote after the war, but also the 42-year-old Polish artist, Jankel Adler, one of whose paintings he bought in 1939,[86] the painter-sculptor, Otto Freundlich (who died in Lublin concentration camp in 1943),[87] the New-Zealander, John Buckland Wright, and the master engraver, Stanley William Hayter, who taught so many famous artists about engraving at his 'Atelier 17' studio in Paris.

    Beckett's trip to Germany in 1936–7 is much better documented now through the discovery after his death of his personal diaries. That visit gave him the chance to see work that was regarded as 'degenerate' by the Nazi regime, as well as to meet local Hamburg painters Eduard Bargheer, Karl Kluth, Willem Grimm and (Beckett's personal

Penelope Wilton, Ronald Pickup and Anna Massey in *Play*, 1976

favourite) Karl Ballmer. At the time many of the 'decadent paintings' were either being removed from the walls, literally as he moved on from city to city, or locked up in cellars and reserve collections, for which a special permit was needed to view them, prior to many of them being sold or destroyed. The modern section of the Kronprinzenpalais in Berlin was closed, for example, in October 1936, shortly before Beckett arrived there from Hamburg and Braunschweig anxious to see the modern art collection. In Halle, an important exhibition of 'Decadent art' was open, but with a separate entrance charge. And on the day that Beckett was in the town he was the sole visitor to the exhibition.

After the war, he was heavily involved in translating books and articles on modern art through regular collaborative work with Georges Duthuit, who introduced him to many painters in the late 1940s and early 1950s. He also helped Ralph Mannheim to translate Duthuit's book, *The Fauvist Painters* (1950). A number of artists figured among his closest friends. Henri Hayden, whom he met during the war in Roussillon in the Vaucluse, when both of them were hiding out from the Nazis – Beckett because he had worked with the Resistance, Hayden because he was Jewish – was one such close friend. Slightly later, another was Avigdor Arikha, whose work he enthusiastically supported and with whom he frequently talked about art and literature. In addition, he knew the sculptor, Alberto Giacometti, who designed the tree for the 1961 Odéon Theatre production of *Waiting for Godot* and with whom he used to have late-night drinks in the boulevard cafés. He was also very friendly with the painters, Joan Mitchell and Jean-Paul Riopelle[88] and knew several less well-known painters, including Sergio de Castro and Robert Pikelny.

The subject of Beckett's relations with modern artists and his debt to modern art is too large to be dealt with at all adequately here. But it is worth noting that some of the devices he adopted for the imagery of his late plays, such as unusual perspective, distortion and fragmentation may be compared with techniques employed by some German Expressionist painters, although they certainly cannot be equated with them. This is scarcely surprising in view of the enthusiasm that Beckett felt, in his thirties, for the painters of the *Brücke* and *Blaue Reiter*. He cannot himself be described as an Expressionist writer. There were too many sides to Expressionism that he could never share: the initial flight of German Expressionist writers into utopianism before the dominant tone, in Expressionist painting in particular, became more anguished and despairing; a stridency and a tendency to grandiloquence, overstatement and what, writing about Karl Schmidt-Rottluff's work, Beckett referred to as 'monumentalism'.[89] *Not I* has, understandably, often been compared with Munch's painting, *The Scream*, and Beckett's private diaries supply convincing evidence of the admiration that he had for some of Munch's work. 'In breakfast room [of a private collector in Hamburg]', he wrote, 'a superb Munch, three women on a bridge over dark water, apparently a frequent motif. Best Munch I have seen.'[90] But, even with Munch, Beckett, too, often found an overstatement and a sentimentality in his paintings that were alien to his own love of the understated.[91] Yet, as Daniel Albright recently stresses,[92] alongside this restraint and understatement there was an inescapable 'cry of pain' side to Beckett, which helps to explain why he was drawn to painters like Munch, Nolde, Schmidt-Rottluff and Marc, although not to the explicit horror of the work of an Otto Dix or the grotesquerie of a George Grosz.

Beckett also admired many of the paintings of Lyonel Feininger and Ernst Ludwig Kirchner, about whom he enthused in his German diaries. If, then, the head of Listener in *That Time* really does owe a debt to William Blake's images of Job or God the Father, as I am sure it does, the perspective adopted is a highly unusual one and may have been transposed from the world of modern art. In the collection of modern paintings that he saw in Halle in 1937, Beckett was most intrigued by the unusual perspectives that he found in some of Feininger's work exhibited there: 'All about 1930, and technique perhaps less interesting than the out-and-out "plane" technique of earlier Feininger, of which some examples here also. Diener is very trouble[d] by some perspectives that are not alas in Nature.'[93] These perspectives did not worry Beckett in the slightest and, when he came to imagine the head of the protagonist in *That Time*, he gave a highly unusual perspective to the stage image: the long, flaring white hair of Listener was

presented 'as if seen from above outspread'; this powerful, floating image is accompanied by a fragmented text that relates a haunting tale of solitude and alienation.[94] In *Not I*, Mouth was placed upstage 'about 8 feet above stage level, faintly lit from close-up and below, rest of face in shadow', while the 'tall standing figure' of the Auditor stood downstage on 'a podium about 4 feet high'.[95] This unusual configuration and contrast of size is reminiscent of the distortions that often characterise Expressionist painting. The simplicity, two-dimensionality, purity of line and emphasis on horizontals and verticals that are found in Kirchner's paintings and the starkness of his dramatically simplified black-and-white woodcuts are aspects of his work that are also worth considering as possible influences on Beckett. One thinks of the use made by Beckett of the vertical tree and the horizontal stone in his own Schiller Theatre production of *Waiting for Godot*. *Come and Go*, with its three women dressed in long violet, red and yellow coats, is reminiscent of a Kirchner painting, such as *Two Women in the Street* (1914) or even *Berlin Street Scene* (1913–14).

It is difficult, then, to look at Beckett's late plays without thinking of some of the features of Kirchner's, Feininger's or Munch's paintings. The focus that Beckett brings to the isolation of whole figures or parts of figures; the alienation of one human being from another; the fragmentation of the human body, with its separation of the head from the rest of a body or the mouth from the head (as in *Play*, *That Time* and *Not I*); the sculptural, spectral quality of the figure of May in *Footfalls*, with its emphasis on what Billie Whitelaw called the 'dinosaur-like pose' of her awkwardly curved, pacing body; the seated, then slow-moving figure in the television play, *Ghost Trio*: all of these elements of Beckett's later stage or television paintings – for that essentially is what, quite knowingly, he was doing – are difficult to imagine without his experience of modern and, more specifically, of Expressionist art.

Although I deal more fully with Beckett's interest in the silent screen in the third essay of this book, it is worth mentioning in this context that he was also very familiar with Expressionist and Surrealist cinema. If *Come and Go*

(*Left*) Natasha Parry in *Oh les beaux jours*, 1998

reminds us of a Kirchner painting, it also echoes the ending of Fritz Lang's famous 1931 film, M. The central image of Winnie, buried up to her waist in the earth, in *Happy Days* may just have originated, as we have seen, in an incident on a holiday beach, but it was probably more likely to have been borrowed from the final frames of Buñuel and Dali's film, *Un chien andalou*, the script of which appeared in the same number of the literary magazine, *This Quarter*, as Beckett's own translations of Eluard and Breton poems.[96] The natural way in which Beckett could draw from his memories of Expressionist cinematographic techniques is shown by an entry in an account in his German diary of a walk that he took under the river in Hamburg: 'by foot to Landsbrücke and through Elbtunnel. Impressive and nightmarish, especially the Fährschächten, pits of steel with 6 lifts each and German expressionist film screw stairs. Whole thing somehow kinematic. Hordes of dockers homeward bound on far side, pouring into lifts and clattering down stairs.'[97] In 1966, Beckett himself became closely involved with the director, Marin Karmitz, in making the film of his play, *Comédie* (Play), which employed many Expressionist devices: 'the dramaturgical use of the spotlight . . . as well as the opposition of light and darkness and the dramatic interplay of shadows',[98] in addition to striking, indeed startling use of close-ups of the human face that owed so much to early cinema. What is clear is that, for Beckett, cinema had its own part to play in the exciting world of modern European art that he discovered for himself in the late 1920s and 1930s, above all in France and Germany.

Beckett put Wassily Kandinsky with Paul Klee, Bram van Velde, Georges Rouault, Georges Braque, Jack Yeats and (more controversially) the Swiss painter, Karl Ballmer, among 'the great of our time'.[99] The statement that Beckett made to John Gruen in an interview published in *Vogue* in which he distinguished himself from Kandinsky and Schoenberg on the issue of formalism and abstraction suggests that he had thought long and hard about what he was doing in relation to modern art and music. 'I think perhaps I have freed myself from certain formal concepts. Perhaps like the composer Schoenberg or the painter Kandinsky, I have turned towards an abstract language. Unlike them, however, I have tried not to concretize the abstraction – not give it yet another formal context.'[100] We should remember that at the time he gave this interview Beckett was struggling to write a series of short prose texts that could reasonably be described as verging on the abstract, and that his remarks did not necessarily project forward to the major prose texts and the plays that were to follow over the next two decades of his life. It partly depends, of course, upon which of the meanings of 'abstract' one is focusing: its non-representational aspect, or its conceptual, as distinct from concrete, material aspect.

The Lost Ones at first appears to follow formal patterns and present a non-representational, invented world. Yet it has within it elements such as the woman (the North) that draw the reader back to human forms. Even a text like Lessness, in which the themes of 'ruin, exposure, wilderness, mindlessness, past and future denied and affirmed'[101] are interwoven, still contains feeble but resilient flickers of being: 'Grey face two pale blue little body heart beating only upright.'[102]

In Beckett's later prose works such as Ill Seen Ill Said, Worstward Ho and Stirrings Still purely local, specific details were removed. Yet in these texts he still managed to avoid 'concretizing the abstract'. Indeed, contrary to most works based on rigid formal patterns, there are almost always elements of Beckett's work that reach out beyond the texts themselves to move, stir, and shock, sometimes even to make one's hair stand on end. Certain passages from his last, linguistically complex text, Worstward Ho, for instance, are deeply moving. One such image is that of an old man walking hand in hand with a child, an image that had haunted Beckett for some fifty years: 'Hand in hand with equal plod they go. In the free hands – no. Free empty hands. Backs turned both bowed with equal plod they go. The child hand raised to reach the old holding hand. Hold the old holding hand. Hold and be held. Plod on and never recede. Slowly with never a pause plod on and never recede. Backs turned. Both bowed. Joined by old holding hands. Plod on as one. One shade. Another shade.'[103] The image of a third figure in the book survives the worsening that is being explored in this text: 'Nothing and yet a

woman. Old and yet old. On unseen knees. Stooped as loving memory some old gravestones stoop. In that old graveyard. Names gone and when to when. Stoop mute over the graves of none.'[104] Language in this text is subject to the most radical of reappraisals; syntax is fractured; grammar is restructured; words reform themselves, newly coined, before our very eyes, taking on unfamiliar shapes – 'unworsenable', 'unmoreable', 'unlessenable', 'meremost', 'dimmost', 'unnullable least'. Yet a hard, spare, vibrant, poetic prose emerges: 'Where in the narrow vast? Say only vasts apart. In that narrow void vasts of voids apart'; 'To last unlessenable least how loath to leasten'.[105] The alliterative technique is familiar enough. Yet Beckett's struggle to resuscitate a language that must inevitably fail – fail to find the right words to express the chaos of being, the fragility of a brief existence, or Pascal's 'silence of infinite space' – is bold, even thrilling.

Looking back on the shorter plays of the 1960s, *Play* could indeed be described, as it was by Marin Karmitz, as a 'Feydeau-like sex story, a very funny story of adultery in which Beckett's talent consisted of breaking reality and placing it in abstraction'.[106] Even here, humour itself, as well as brief glimpses of human feeling, play against both the patterns and the Limbo-like setting. And in the later short plays, with a few exceptions such as *Quad* and *What Where*, Beckett seems to have recoiled from the temptations of abstraction to blend concreteness, directness and vibrancy of the image with fragility and evanescence. What also happened is that, by isolating and concentrating the image, he managed to create a distillation of feeling: the inevitable sadness and anticipated death of the three friends meeting again in *Come and Go* – and this already in a play from the 1960s; the loss, absence and distress encapsulated in *Footfalls*; the sense of isolation and alienation conveyed by *Not I*; the resignation found in *Rockaby*; the resilience and revolt expressed in *Catastrophe*. The formal, almost mathematical patterning that forms an important part of many of these plays, works then not, as one might suppose it would, away from human feeling but draws one towards it.

As someone who (to my acute embarrassment) found himself bursting into tears at a dress rehearsal of *Footfalls*, I find the notion of Beckett as an arid, inhuman formalist extremely difficult to accept. It is, moreover, precisely this particular blend of reduction, concentration and distillation with the intricate patterning and repetition of words, gestures and movements that has made Beckett into such a major influence on modern painters and on video and installation artists.

(*Left*) Billie Whitelaw rehearsing *Footfalls*, 1976

Beckett as director

Samuel Beckett was closely involved with the staging of his plays from the very outset of his career as a dramatist. He attended almost all of the rehearsals of the first (and original) French production of *En attendant Godot* (*Waiting for Godot*) in the latter months of 1952, when he acted discreetly as an advisor to its director, Roger Blin. He also helped Blin, with much greater self-assurance this time around, to direct the world première of *Fin de partie* (*Endgame*) in 1957. Yet it was to be almost ten years more before he began to direct his own productions. Throughout this period, however, he helped and advised several other experienced English and French directors – George Devine, Donald McWhinnie, Anthony Page and Jean-Marie Serreau – with productions of *Endgame*, *Krapp's Last Tape*, *Happy Days*, and *Play*, as well as assisting with a number of revivals of *Godot*. In that time, he learned all that he possibly could about staging and lighting from these directors, who became personal friends. Occasionally, he was invited to come in to bale out a production that had run into choppy waters.[1] Then, from the mid-1960s on, he directed almost all of his own stage and television plays at least once, until his career as a director came to an end at the ripe old age of 80 with a production of *Was Wo* (*What Where*) for German television.

Why did he choose to direct his own plays? With a few notable exceptions, most playwrights in the past have preferred not to do this, although it has become much more common in recent years. Beckett directed partly because he was asked to do so. The Schiller Theatre administration in Berlin, the Royal Court Theatre in London and the Compagnie Renaud-Barrault in Paris were responsible for inviting him to take sole charge of productions. From personal encounters and reports of his wife and friends on productions done by others,[2] as well as from photographs, recordings and reviews, he had become aware that some of them were falling far short of his expectations. He told Michael Haerdter, his assistant on the 1967 Schiller Theatre *Endgame*, for instance, 'I saw photographs of the first Berlin production; everything is wrong in it. The ash bins are separated, you can see Hamm's feet, they're touching the ground.'[3] He was also sharply critical of

(*Left*) Samuel Beckett directing Billie Whitelaw in *Footfalls*, 1976

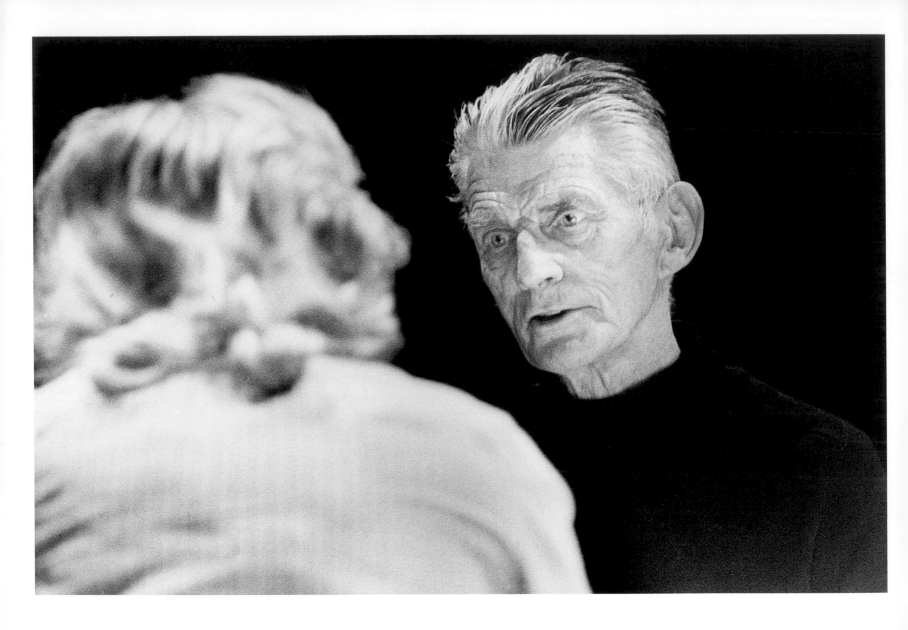

certain aspects of the first English production of *Waiting for Godot*, when he attended several performances at the Criterion Theatre in London with the American director, Alan Schneider.[4] Schneider wrote in his autobiography, *Entrances*, 'my fondest memories are of Beckett's clutching my arm from time to time and, in a clearly heard stage whisper, saying, 'It's ahl wrahng! He's doing it ahl wrahng!' about a particular bit of stage business or the interpretation of a certain line. He particularly erupted when the Boy at the end of the second act pointed to the heavens when he was asked by Vladimir where Mr Godot lived.'[5] He mocked what he called this 'Anglican fervour'.[6]

It was not that he felt there was only one way of doing his work. 'I don't claim my interpretation is the only correct one', he said to Haerdter. 'It's possible to do the play quite differently, different music, movements, different rhythm, the kitchen can be differently located and so on.'[7] But we should not exaggerate his tolerance. He was dismayed, annoyed, even infuriated at times when he learned of directors making very obvious mistakes or – especially, he felt, in Germany – taking gross liberties with his work. They were, as he saw it, distorting his vision and he could become fiercely and picturesquely eloquent about such extravagant productions. He wrote to Alan Schneider, for instance: 'I dream sometimes of all German directors of plays with perhaps one exception united in one with his back to the wall and me shooting a bullet into his balls every five minutes till he loses his taste for improving authors.'[8] (Schneider, by the way, almost as picturesquely, used to call such directors members of 'the flashing-lights school of directors'.) Nevertheless, in his calmer moments, Beckett recognised how much staging the plays with different actors and in different theatres inevitably changed a work. The cuts and changes that he himself made in his different productions of the same play also contradict the view that he believed that any definitive staging was possible. But for him there was a huge difference between a faithful interpretation and a distortion, let alone a travesty.

As Beckett became more experienced and more confident of himself as a director, he wanted to try out his latest plays on the stage for himself. He felt

(*Left*) Samuel Beckett directing Billie Whitelaw in *Happy Days*, 1979

that this was particularly necessary with the late, delicate, highly condensed, experimental dramas such as *Not I*, *That Time* or *Footfalls*, in which he consciously felt that he was testing the limits of what was thought possible in the theatre. But he also hoped to correct what he regarded as deficiencies in the stagecraft of his earlier plays. He always maintained, for instance, that he had written *Waiting for Godot* at a time when he was ignorant about the theatre (the play was 'messy', he told Ruby Cohn[9]) and that many things in it could, and should, be improved. Once he had discovered how much directing the plays could reveal about them even to himself, he came to regard their staging as an important, continuing phase of the creative process, not as something separate from it. As early as November 1963, he wrote to Alan Schneider about his new work, *Play*: 'I realise that no final script is possible till I have had work on rehearsals'[10] and, increasingly, this came to be the attitude that he adopted towards all the plays that followed.

Part of the attraction of directing his own work was also that it allowed him not only to 'get right' what was written down, but also to work with what could not be expressed on the printed page: the echoes or contrasts of balancing or differing voices, using them like musical instruments; the tone and pitch of an inflexion; the precision and shape of gesture; the quality of a look; the frequency and duration of a silence or a pause; the direction, speed and manner of a stage move; the pace and rhythms of a section of dialogue, or even, in the case of *Play* or *Not I*, of an entire play. It also offered him the opportunity to relate these different elements to dramatic themes that perhaps only he could fully identify.

Although Beckett welcomed the opportunity to realise his personal vision more fully on the stage, he always had a curious love–hate relationship with the theatre. He loathed all the fuss that surrounds theatrical events, the social dimension of theatre-going, the pressures to meet a first-night deadline, and the need for publicity for the sake of the theatre and the production – although, in later years, in Britain, France and Germany, the news that he was directing one of his plays was usually enough to guarantee both ticket sales and press coverage. On the other hand, although he found the rehearsal process challenging and exhausting, he also found it deeply compelling. It appealed to his strong practical sense and real interest in theatrical technicalities.

Rehearsals were fascinating affairs whenever Beckett was directing. He quickly established a working atmosphere of intense concentration. His relations with the actors were quiet, formal, friendly and courteous. Nonetheless, even with actors who were close personal friends, like Patrick Magee or Jack MacGowran, with whom he would be totally at ease sitting in a pub with a glass of Guinness in his hand, he found it hard not to be tense as they worked intensively on one of his plays. Michael Haerdter described the ambience at rehearsals of *Endgame* in Berlin as one of 'intense objectivity, earnest and at times rather precarious tension'.[11] Walter Asmus, Beckett's German assistant on the later production of *Waiting for Godot*, defined this rather as a 'relaxed tension'.[12] 'It's ahl difficult' was a phrase that Beckett used several times to me about the rehearsal situation. He usually got on extremely well with the technical staff of the theatre, whom he consulted regularly and respected for their specialist know-how. Many of them became his most devoted fans and friends, who would walk through fire for him.

His approach to directing actors was essentially pragmatic. He would help them to discover the right tone for a particular speech, even for a single phrase, often picking up with strict musical precision the tone already adopted for another phrase. Sometimes he would read through an entire passage himself to illustrate exactly how he thought it should be delivered. Occasionally, he would go on to the stage to try out the patterns or the timing of certain moves or gestures. Billie Whitelaw wrote in her autobiography, *Billie Whitelaw . . . Who He?* of how, one day during a lunch break from rehearsals of *Happy Days*, she 'was standing in the wings watching Sam, a long, thin figure without an ounce of spare flesh on him, crawling round the mound of earth on the stage. That entire lunch hour he spent in deep, deep concentration, playing Willie, crawling round and round.'[13] In general, he encouraged his actors to find simple, exact, concrete and economical actions. 'Economy' was a key word for Beckett, since, as we shall see later, he equated this with maximum grace. Patrick Magee said that his greatest contribution

at rehearsals was to make everything appear clear and simple, and other actors whom Beckett directed spoke of how invaluable and reassuring it was to have him there, whenever a difficult line or an awkward move came up.[14]

He scarcely ever discussed questions of meaning, however, with the performers. In letters about *Endgame* to Alan Schneider, he was happy enough to write to his director friend about the relevance of the arguments of the Sophists to the play. Yet he warned Schneider, 'Don't mention any of this to your actors!'[15] To the actors in the German *Endgame* at the Schiller Theatre, he said: 'I don't want to talk about my play; it has to be taken purely dramatically to take shape on the stage. There's nothing in it about philosophy – maybe about poetry. Here the only interest of the play is as dramatic material.'[16] When Gudrun Genest asked Beckett whether Nell, the character she was playing, really did die in her bin, he replied, hiding behind an ironic disclaimer of special knowledge, 'So it seems, but no one knows.'[17] Even with Magee and MacGowran, when they were rehearsing *Endgame* in London, he pleaded ignorance of the wider implications of his text: 'I only know what's on the page' he says with a friendly gesture, 'Do it your way.'[18]

At rehearsals, he deliberately shied away from discussing ideas. Yet, watching him direct his plays or talking to him privately, it was obvious – in spite of his comment to the actors – that he was acutely aware of the philosophical issues, hidden resonances and ambiguities that are deeply embedded in his writing. 'The play is full of echoes', he admitted to the German cast of *Endgame*, 'they all answer each other'.[19] Directing his own work, he concentrated on picking up these echoes. But he treated them, as he promised he would, purely as *dramatic* material, as elements in a complex poetic and musical structure.

Rather than talk in abstract concepts, what Beckett tended to do with actors was to find simple, concrete images to convey essential truths about the character or the situation. In this way, he was able, without discussing questions of meaning, to provide them with hooks on which they could hang their performances. 'Winnie has something bird-like about her, something

(*Left*) Leonard Fenton and Billie Whitelaw in *Happy Days*, 1979

that belongs to the air', he said, for example, to Eva-Katarina Schultz about *Happy Days*,[20] adding later that she was 'a bird with oil on its feathers'.[21] To Rick Cluchey, who played Krapp in his English production of *Krapp's Last Tape* in Berlin, Beckett described the character as 'a tiger in his cage'; 'he's a loner eaten up with himself'.[22] To Ernst Schroeder, who played Hamm in the Schiller Theatre production of *Endgame*, he said: 'He's a king in this chess match lost-from-the-start.'[23] *Endgame*, he said to the German actors, is 'like "fire and ashes"'; 'Hamm and Clov . . . are both focused on quiet and inner contemplation, but one of them is always disturbing the other; the other is always the peace-breaker, and fire suddenly flares out of the ashes of quietness.'[24]

Even with someone like Alan Schneider, with whom Beckett was usually so open in letters and private conversation, he was reluctant to talk discursively about his work and preferred to talk practicalities. Writing about their early conversations concerning *Waiting for Godot*, the American director wrote:

> I plied him with some of my studiously prepared questions as well as all the ones that came to me at the moment. He tried to answer as directly and as honestly as he could. I discovered that Beckett was perfectly willing to answer any question that was specific, a specific meaning or reference. He would not – and would never – go into larger or symbolic meanings, preferring his work to speak for itself and letting the supposed 'meanings' fall where they might.[25]

It is clear, from these and many other examples, that, although fascinated by ideas, Beckett considered any discussion of them at rehearsal as out of place, unnecessary, even positively distracting. He also obviously felt that ideas should never draw attention to themselves in productions, which should be more concerned with poetry and with drama. Poetry was always very important to him,[26] but, in this case, it was poetry in a dramatic context.

There is clear evidence that Beckett was interested as early as the mid-1930s in the somewhat uneasy relationship that exists between poetry and the theatre. If we exclude an unfinished fragment about Dr Johnson, this was over ten years before he wrote a play himself. During his stay in Germany in 1936–7, in Berlin, he went to see the actor Werner Krauss, starring in Hebbel's poetic tragedy of jealousy and sexual tension, *Gyges und sein Ring* (*Gyges and his Ring*) (1856). Afterwards, in his private diary, he set down his objections to 'poetical drama': 'the poetical play', he wrote, 'can never come off as play, nor when played as poetry either, because the words obscure the action and are obscured by it'.[27] He went on to argue in a letter to an Irish friend, Mary Manning, that the Hebbel 'play is such good poetry that it never comes alive at all', poetic speeches being 'too self-sufficient to be merely phases of a dramatic expression'.[28] Interestingly, in his diary he went on to compare the poetic drama of Hebbel and the theatre of Racine (on whom he had given a course of lectures at Trinity College, Dublin, and of whom he was a great admirer). Racine, he claimed, 'never elaborates the expression in this sense, never stands by the word in this sense, and therefore his plays are not "poetical" i.e. undramatic in this sense'.[29]

In the late 1940s and early 1950s poetic drama in English meant verse drama like Christopher Fry's *A Phoenix Too Frequent* (1946) and *The Lady's Not for Burning* (1948) or T. S. Eliot's *The Cocktail Party* (1949) and the earlier *Murder in the Cathedral* (1935). In French (although most of their plays were not written in actual verse form), it meant the drama of Jean Vauthier, Jacques Audiberti, Paul Claudel, even Jean Giraudoux. Whether in verse or in prose, the dominant form of expression in these plays was a lyrical, poeticised, often purely decorative form of language. There are, of course, many memorable passages in Beckett's own plays that could be described as 'poetic' in a conventional sense: Pozzo's tirade on time, for example, 'They give birth astride of a grave, the light gleams an instant, then it's night once more',[30] or Vladimir and Estragon's beautifully patterned, lyrical exchanges, 'All the dead voices. / They make a noise like wings. / Like leaves. / Like sand. / Like leaves.'[31] But Beckett felt that the theatre should be poetic in a deeper sense than this, and the poetry in his plays is usually integral to the dramatic situation. In *Waiting for Godot*, for instance, the dramatic action is reduced to near stasis and a poetic metaphor is made of the central waiting situation. In *Endgame* the characters slowly enact the difficulty of 'ending' in a drama that

manages to be at once concrete and suggestive. In *Krapp's Last Tape* the poetry does not primarily arise out of Krapp's lyrical accounts of his experience with a woman in the punt or the death of his mother, however touching these may be, but from the direct encounter between a man and his recorded past, a fascinating conjunction of like and unlike.

When Beckett turned to direct his own plays, he aimed above all to create a unified, musically organised, poetic structure. It is quite possible that he simply evolved his own methods of directing as a result of a combination of impulse and experience. His usual practice, however, was to read widely, then to think deeply about the literary or theatrical problems involved before coming up with his own solutions. He had already done this in the early 1930s in the case of the novel, before writing, first, the posthumously published *Dream of Fair to Middling Women* and then *Murphy* (1938).

There is, as yet, no real evidence to prove that Beckett read Edward Gordon Craig's *The Art of Theatre*, although this seems very likely. There is much in Craig's writings on the theatre that finds either an echo or a parallel in Beckett's own practice as a director.[32] Beckett would certainly have discovered in *The Art of Theatre* an important distinction between a theatre of words, of literature, and a truly poetic theatre that incorporated all the different elements of theatrical art. 'The art of the theatre', wrote Craig, 'is neither

John Hurt in *Krapp's Last Tape*, 1999

acting nor the play; it is not scene or dance, but it consists of all the elements of which these things are composed: action, which is the very spirit of acting; words, which are the body of the play; line and colour which are the very heart of the scene; rhythm, which is the very essence of dance.'[33] If it were not in Craig that he found this emphasis on total theatre, then he would certainly have found it eloquently announced in Antonin Artaud's *The Theatre and its Double*, which we know he read – 'for the occasional blaze' was the way he put it to me.[34] Artaud argued that the theatre was not a branch of spoken language but that it should be allowed to speak its own solid, material language. 'I maintain', he wrote, 'that this physical language, aimed at the senses and independent of speech, must first satisfy the senses. There must be poetry for the senses just as there is for speech.'[35] And he went on to say that 'true poetry is metaphysical and I might even say it is its metaphysical scope, its degree of metaphysical effectiveness, which gives it its proper value'.[36] Beckett went on to create his own kind of poetic and metaphysical theatre – in Jean Cocteau's words, penned as early as 1922 – a 'poésie de théâtre' (poetry of the theatre), to be distinguished from 'la poésie au théâtre' (poetry in the theatre).[37]

There were differences between Beckett and Craig on a number of issues. Beckett would have rejected, for example, Craig's contention that gesture and poetry had nothing to do with each

Conor Lovett in *Act Without Words I*, 1999

other, just as he would certainly have disapproved of Craig's notion that the author was 'poaching' on the preserves of the director if he provided detailed stage directions to accompany his text. Beckett, on the other hand, wanted to envision and set down as much as he possibly could about the visuals of his plays. Yet, in other key respects, he was extremely close to Craig, especially on questions to do with acting and what it should and should not be. Denis Bablet wrote: 'Craig's final bugbear is realism on the stage. His whole work and everything he has written are a reiterated protest against the clumsy, blatant, direct imitation of reality. The actor must not be content to record like a camera, to reproduce appearances, to copy nature, instead of creating with the aid of nature.'[38]

In terms of acting style, Beckett also eschewed naturalism. 'He was determined to avoid imitation of reality,' commented David Bradby, 'but he respected the real tensions, desires and frustrations present in the ways people interrelate.'[39] Within this broad framework, he tried to promote in his actors an acting style that was appropriate to the vision of each of his plays, not one that slavishly imitated reality. *Waiting for Godot*, for instance, with its close links with *commedia dell'arte*, music hall and silent screen, was played by the German actors under his direction as meticulously choreographed, balletic vaudeville. 'It is a game', Beckett said to the actors, 'everything is a game. When all four of them are lying on the ground, that cannot be handled naturalistically. That has got to be done artificially, balletically. Otherwise everything becomes an imitation, an imitation of reality.'[40] In his German production of *Endgame*, the actors playing Hamm and Clov were instructed to bring out the dark humour in the play in sometimes rapid-fire, non-naturalistic dialogue, in which rhythm and pace mattered just as much as what was being said: 'There must be maximum aggression between them from the first exchange of words onward', said Beckett, 'Their war is the nucleus of the play.'[41] For his 1979 Royal Court Theatre, London production of *Happy Days*, he encouraged a quality of strangeness in Billie Whitelaw's acting that reflected his perception of Winnie as 'a bit mad. Manic is not wrong, but too big . . . A child woman with a short span of concentration – sure one minute, unsure the next'; 'she's scatterbrained, she babbles', he added.[42] This strange, almost manic quality affected the sudden, eagle-like, swooping gestures that were adopted by the actress, as well as the speed, tone and pitch of her delivery. In the later *Not I*, Whitelaw's acting of Mouth was rapid, almost breathless, while, in *Footfalls*, Beckett worked with the same actress to convey a ghostly absence, where her words appeared as frail and as insubstantial as her physical presence. There was, of course, the danger that his methods would lead to an excess of stylisation, a danger that, as a director, he kept very much in mind. He embraced artificiality and yet he worked hard to avoid anything that appeared forced, rigid or sterile.

Beckett's (privately stated) attitudes towards the actor also have much in common with Craig's related views on the *über-marionette*. Craig explained in the preface to the 1925 edition of *On the Art of the Theatre* that 'the *über-marionette* is the actor plus fire, minus egoism; the fire of the gods and demons, without the smoke and steam of mortality'.[43] Craig also wrote that 'the actor must cease to express *himself* and begin to express something else; he must no longer imitate, he must *indicate* . . . Then his acting will become impersonal, he will lose his "egoism" and use his body and voice as though they were materials rather than parts of himself. To this end a symbolical style of acting most be devised, based on the power of the creative imagination.'[44] Many actors and directors who worked with Beckett spoke of his personal dislike of what is so often thought of as acting and of his tendency to dehumanise the actors in his plays. Brenda Bruce, who played Winnie in the British première of *Happy Days*, told me how he tried to get her to speak her lines according to a very strict rhythm and in a very flat tone. To her horror, one day, he even brought a metronome into the theatre and set it down on the floor; 'this is the rhythm I want you to follow', he said, leaving it to tick inexorably away. Siân Phillips also spoke about Beckett's insistence on rhythm and tonelessness when she was rehearsing her recording of the voice for his television play, *Eh Joe*, with him. 'We worked like machines,' she said, 'beating time with our fingers',[45] until eventually she managed to get somewhere close to the flat, cold, toneless voice that he could hear in his head.

It seems likely that both Craig and Beckett found a common inspiration for their approach in Heinrich von Kleist's essay, 'Über das

Marionettentheater', which Craig had published in English in *The Marionette* in 1918 and which Beckett much admired.[46] This essay offers a perfectly logical explanation of what they wanted to achieve with the actor in the theatre. According to Kleist's speaker, puppets possess a mobility, symmetry, harmony and grace greater than any human dancer can ever have. For, inevitably, the puppet lacks self-awareness, hence affectation, which is what destroys natural grace and charm in man. Man is a creature permanently off balance. In an actor's performance, based as it so often is on imitation, self-consciousness (or in Craig's words 'egoism') almost inevitably breaks through. Beckett too found this intrusive and antipathetic. His aim was to achieve an authenticity of being that had nothing to do with the 'living-into' the role by the actor extolled by Stanislavski. A dependence on imitation went diametrically against the economy of movement and gesture that Beckett was aiming for in order to attain a harmony and grace that had more to do with what Craig called 'a living spirit' than with any direct imitation of life.

When such an unusual view of the actor's role was combined with Beckett's own dual position as author and director, it is hardly surprising that it created problems for him. A clash between the two roles sometimes introduced an element of sharp tension that adversely affected the relations between him and the actors with whom he was working. Problems arose at times because of changes that Beckett had made in his text. This was the case when he was directing his favourite actress, Billie Whitelaw, in *Happy Days* in 1979. As Whitelaw delivered the lines, he put his hand to his brow and groaned audibly whenever she made mistakes in a text that, most unhelpfully one has to say, he had revised since she had learned it, transforming, for example, 'Oh well' into 'Ah well', 'What now' into 'And now', and so on. His reactions naturally disturbed Billie Whitelaw dreadfully. Beckett for his part was aware that he was upsetting her but seemed quite incapable of doing anything about it. Since I had been at rehearsal and had witnessed the unfortunate incidents, Whitelaw telephoned me in the evening to ask me whether I would ask him to stop. My answer was: 'I don't think he can stop.' She then phoned Dame

Peggy Ashcroft, telling her that Beckett was driving her mad and asking her what she could possibly do. Ashcroft's reply was: 'You've got to ask him to leave, dear . . . he's impossible.'[47] The situation became so distressing for both Beckett and Whitelaw that he was asked – at a hastily convened dinner party at the house of Stuart Burge, the Royal Court's artistic director, with Beckett's friends, Jocelyn Herbert and Donald McWhinnie – to absent himself from rehearsals for a few days until Whitelaw's shattered self-confidence could be gradually rebuilt.[48]

More often, however, difficulties arose out of conflicts as to what Beckett wanted and how the actor or actress was going to arrive there. Even when only acting as advisor to the director, Sir Peter Hall, with Dame Peggy Ashcroft as Winnie in the National Theatre production in 1974, he made himself deeply unpopular with the actress, just as he had done with Brenda Bruce, by (among other things) wanting her to play Winnie in a flat, monotonous, unemotional style. As Hall wrote in his diaries, an actress like Dame Peggy needed to feel everything strongly at first, in order to be able to hide it (or express it more subtly) later.

> But the slightest sign of feeling disturbs Sam, and he speaks of his need for monotony, paleness, weakness. This is where, unlike Harold [Pinter], he is not finally a theatre worker, great director though he can be. He confuses the work process with the result. I suppose it's

Pat Kinevane in *Act Without Words II*, 1999

understandable. A writer of his meticulousness must achieve the phrase he wants very quickly as he sets it down on paper, otherwise he crosses it out. But an actor takes weeks of work to explore and then realise a few minutes of text.[49]

In addition, I remember the adamant manner in which Dame Peggy told me that she and Peter Hall were *certainly not* going to accept the cut of an entire page of text that Beckett wanted them to make in the scene in which Winnie's parasol goes on fire. And they did not. Beckett also became frustrated with the awkwardness of working through another director and annoyed by his differences of view with Dame Peggy. Meeting me after a rehearsal, he spoke of inventing reasons for leaving early and returning to Paris.[50]

The problem derived largely, as Peter Hall suggested, from a failure on Beckett's part to appreciate properly the difficulties that an actor or actress encountered as he or she worked towards a performance. Beckett was also concerned, sometimes too early, with reproducing the voice that he heard in his head. Curiously, when faced with the finished product, he often admired some of the very things that at earlier rehearsals he might well have taken out. He never liked emotionalism in his plays. But when emotion was used discreetly and when, perhaps in the wake of the *über-marionette*, it was scrupulously controlled, he could accept, even applaud a performance that incorporated his rhythmical principles but provided a wider emotional range than he had originally envisaged, or maybe even thought possible or desirable. As his favourite stage designer, Jocelyn Herbert, suggested to me, Madeleine Renaud's Winnie in *Oh les beaux jours*, for instance, offered precisely those qualities that Beckett had objected to in the case of Brenda Bruce – human, lyrical and moving. Yet Beckett adored it. Patrick Magee and Billie Whitelaw in England, Jean Martin and Roger Blin in France and Horst Bollmann, Stefan Wigger, Ernst Schroeder and even Martin Held in Germany were other actors who gave him far more than he asked for, inventing and bringing that indispensable spark of genius to their performances. For, with Beckett, as with anyone else, what he wanted in theory was not necessarily

(*Left*) Madeleine Renaud in *Oh les beaux jours*, 1969

what worked most successfully in practice. One should add that, if he did not like the voice of an actor or actress, all was lost from the start.

What, then, were the chief characteristics of Beckett's approach to directing? He was in certain respects a very old-fashioned kind of director who prepared everything meticulously well in advance, spending weeks, even months, committing his text to memory (so that he hardly ever needed to consult the script at rehearsal) and visualising every minute detail of the production. In the early plays, in which the actors could still move relatively normally around the stage, he literally blocked out almost every move they made in his theatrical notebooks.

His rigour and precision were legendary. The theatrical notebooks provide evidence of his enormous concentration and careful, obsessive, almost pedantic visualisation of every moment of the play. The one devoted to *Godot*, for example, prepared as usual before rehearsals began and then amended as they went along, has dozens of lists of repetitions, repetitions with variations, *wartestellen* or waiting moments, detailed sketches of moves, arrows to indicate the direction of these moves, changes of voice and tone, synchronisation of the text with the moves, and parallels and echoes between different moments of the play. One of the consequences of all this intricately detailed preparatory work was that every element of the production fitted into Beckett's overall conception of the play. Nothing was overlooked; nothing was gratuitous or superfluous; nothing was dissonant.

At rehearsals, however, he was not inflexible or impractical as a director. He never insisted on doing things precisely as he had previously imagined them. On the contrary (in spite of the occasional clash on the issue of tone, rhythm and emotion), he showed himself to be keenly aware of the strengths and the limitations of an actor or actress and also of the practical difficulties that a particular stage space could create. He welcomed suggestions from his actors as to how something might be done and was willing to abandon his own ideas if they proved too complex or unduly intellectual. His notebooks contain many erasures, once with 'unrealisable' written across the page, and many amendments and, so, as a result, the finished production did not

Albert Finney in *Krapp's Last Tape*, 1973

always correspond in detail to the blocking of his initial notes.

He was also willing to allow something unforeseen to develop during rehearsals that could change what he had originally planned, provided it seemed right and fitted into his overall view of the play. In *Krapp's Last Tape*, for example, the lamp that hung low over Krapp's table was once set swinging accidentally by the actor playing Krapp. Noting how effective this alternation of light and dark proved to be, Beckett retained it in later productions. He also adopted a new ending for the play (as early as the original London production), with the light of the tape recorder glowing on in the darkness for some time after all the stage lighting had been dimmed.[51] He described that particular discovery to me as 'an accident, heaven sent' and kept it in all future productions.[52]

One unusual aspect of Beckett's directing was his insistence that action and speech should be separated as much as possible. 'Never let your changes of position and voice come together', he advised the actors in his Schiller Theatre production of *Endgame*. 'First comes (a) the altered bodily stance; after it, following a slight pause, comes (b) the corresponding utterance.'[53] This dualistic separation of speech from action was the logical extension of a view of the world that saw it in terms of uncomfortable opposites, but, as a guiding principle for work in the theatre, it might appear to be quite alien to the dramatic stage.

Billie Whitelaw in *Footfalls*, 1976

Nonetheless, it led to some interesting and positive theatrical results. It encouraged, for instance, the emphasis that Beckett wanted to place on the image and the 'frozen tableau', while not distracting from the intricate patterns of visual and auditory echoes that he consistently wove into his directing. As S. E. Gontarski explained, it 'suggest[ed] a series of still pictures or photographs more than continuous action or movement'.[54] In this respect, taken along with Beckett's initial choice of often startling images, it served to bring the visual elements of his plays into a much closer relationship with photography and film or the arts of painting and sculpture than most productions of plays normally achieve. Before examining more closely the principles that Beckett followed in directing his own plays, it may be helpful – since we have already looked at the impact that painting had on his work in the theatre – to see how his long-standing interest in film influenced him as a director.

From his early youth, Beckett went regularly, often with his brother, Frank, and his Uncle Howard, to various cinemas in Dublin and to a little cinema in Kingstown (the present Dún Laoghaire). The cinemas of the time showed, of course, silent films and Beckett became a great fan of the comics Buster Keaton, Charlie Chaplin, Ben Turpin and Harry Langdon. His interest in film persisted throughout the 1930s with the advent of sound and colour, and, as his letters and private diaries show, during those years he often went to the cinema in Dublin, London, Paris and Germany. But his enthusiasm for the possibilities of the silent film was to remain undiminished over many decades. In 1936, discussing the first feature film that was made in three-colour Technicolor, *Becky Sharp*, he wrote to his friend, Tom MacGreevy, that its failure in Dublin 'does not encourage my hope that the industrial film will become so completely naturalistic, in stereoscopic colour and gramophonic sound, that a backwater may be created for the two-dimensional silent film that had barely emerged from its rudiments when it was swamped. Then there would be two separate things and no question of a fight between them, or rather of a rout.'[55] Almost thirty years later, invited by Barney Rosset of Grove Press to write a film script for

Evergreen Theater, Beckett produced his own intriguing variant on the silent film, *Film*, with his former idol, Buster Keaton, as the protagonist, in which a surprising 'sshh' is the only sound that is heard throughout the entire film.

In January 1936, Beckett borrowed from a Dublin film buff books by the Russsian film maker, V. I. Pudovkin, and the theorist, Rudolf Arnheim, in addition to copies of the magazine, *Close-up*, which contained articles by Sergei Eisenstein.[56] Combined with his enduring interest in cinema, this reading appears to have inspired Beckett to consider carving out a possible career for himself in film. Soon after, he wrote to Eisenstein at the Moscow State Institute of Cinematography asking the famous director if he would 'take him on',[57] serious in his intentions to become (at the very least) a cameraman or a film editor.[58] There was also a personal connection in that Eisenstein had met Beckett's friend and mentor, James Joyce, several times in Paris and was a great fan of *Ulysses*.[59]

Beckett clearly read Pudovkin's essays on film technique, with their detailed discussions of editing practices, for he wrote to MacGreevy: 'What I would learn under a person like Pudovkin is how to handle a camera, the higher trucs of the editing bench, and so on, of which I know as little as of quantity surveying',[60] the latter being his late father's and his brother's profession. As late as February 1938, shortly after he was stabbed by a pimp in the street in Paris, he was still toying with the idea of working in films, as another letter to MacGreevy suggested: 'Nino Frank was there [in Joyce's apartment]. He may put me in touch with film people here, if by any chance I ever feel like being in touch with anything again.'[61] In the event, nothing came of his approach to Eisenstein and it was his keen interest in film theory, and especially in montage or 'constructive editing', that was to make an important contribution to his future career – but as a playwright and a director, not as a film maker.

In the letter in which he told MacGreevy that he had written to Eisenstein, Beckett also wrote: 'I have read Pudovkin's new book and disliked it.'[62] The 'new book' was almost certainly the film director's lectures, entitled *Film Acting*, which had just been published in English. What he disliked about this book, from the director of films like *The Mother* (1926) and *Storm over Asia*

(1928),[63] was probably its emphasis on realism in both stage and film acting, with the actor 'living-into his role' (à la Stanislavski), as well as its didactic, propagandist perspective. Pudovkin clearly appealed to Beckett as an editor rather than as an authority on acting. The Russian's discussions of 'rhythmic composition' as a principle of film editing would have interested him most of all.

More fascinating still for a budding film maker, however, was Rudolf Arnheim's extensive discussion of film montage and some of Eisenstein's early essays. Arnheim sets out in great detail in his book entitled *Film* (1933) the principles of crosscutting, offering many examples from the films of Pudovkin, Eisenstein, Keaton, Chaplin, the French Surrealists and René Clair. The different categories that he discussed include sequential, interlaced and cut-in montage of a sequence, montage within an individual scene, similarity or contrast of form, movement (a slow movement following a very fast one), subject matter, objects, and so on. Then there are interesting discussions of what Arnheim broadly called 'Time Conditions' and 'Conditions of Space'.[64] The relationship between Beckett's own theatre and early cinema, especially the issue of montage, is a fruitful subject that has only recently begun to be explored by critics.[65] I want to touch here only on a few aspects that appear to be relevant to his practice as a director.

Krapp's Last Tape, although concerned with a man *listening* to a recording made by himself at a much earlier point in time, displays many of the characteristics that Arnheim wrote about with respect to visual pictures. Under the category of 'Time Conditions', the film theorist wrote of 'Before, after', speaking of whole scenes that are cut-in from the past or of scenes that will happen in the future (what he called 'past time' and 'future time'). Beckett's entire play consists of just such a montage in the first sense, in which the old man is *seen* physically present, listening to his own voice recorded thirty years earlier, which is commenting on yet another, even earlier version of himself. Although the medium is sound, the technique of inter-cutting is much the same. Moreover, the tape recording itself contains what Arnheim put into a separate sub-category of 'Before, after' that is 'a succession of details which succeed one another in time within the whole action'.[66] Replaying the recording of thirty years before, Krapp moves, then, through several different moments of his past life, as well as a number of different places in space: the death of his mother; the scene with the girl in the punt; the episode of the revelation on the jetty. Unity is conferred on these scenes by common themes and common imagery. There is a strong visual quality to the recordings, too, that may well owe something to Beckett's interest in cinema and the thinking that lay behind montage. Arnheim wrote about how different shots can be connected over time or space by the subject matter, and offered an example from a film, *The Lower Rhinelanders*, in which a round hillock echoed the same shape as the rounded belly of a student.[67] In the scene that Krapp relates of waiting for his mother to die, he speaks in similar fashion of 'One dark young beauty I recollect particularly, all white and starch, incomparable bosom, with a big black hooded perambulator, most funereal thing.'[68] The images are brought together here by the common subject matter (birth and death) and by the visual shape of the woman and the pram (bosom and hood), as well as by the sharp contrasts of black and white.

Beckett's interest in the striking effects that could be achieved in black-and-white photography and cinema, even his reading of Rudolf Arnheim's essay on film in 1936, may, incidentally, have been partly responsible for his faithfulness to black and white. Arnheim wrote: 'the reduction of actual colour values to a one-dimensional grey series (ranging from pure white to dead black) is a welcome divergence from nature that renders possible the making of decorative pictures rich in intellectual significance by means of light and shade'.[69] 'Decorative pictures' would have seemed to Beckett a trite way of describing the startling contrasts that black and white could render possible but the 'rich intellectual significance' would certainly have sounded a chord in someone who was to go on to explore in his own work both the intellectual and the suggestive pictorial possibilities of black-and-white imagery.

As he directed *Krapp's Last Tape*, Beckett was concerned not only, as we shall see in more detail later, with establishing a complex web of black-and-white images, but also with organising and timing the various montage sequences. He worked, for instance, with the various actors who played Krapp under his direction to distinguish clearly the younger voice from the older one, and his theatrical notes focus on how the Krapp we see on stage reacts in contrasting ways to the different subjects, moods and tones of the tape recording. With *Krapp's Last Tape*, Beckett created, then, an apparently simple but actually rather complex play that uses mixed sound and vision and puts into operation some of the principles of montage outlined by Arnheim. Directing it, he must have felt at times that he was not far from fulfilling some of his youthful ambitions, although in a different medium.

Several of Beckett's other plays use the principle of inter-cutting (either auditory or visual or a mixture of both) in a variety of ways. The most striking of these is *That Time*, which inter-cuts three different voice tracks relating to different periods in the life history of the protagonist. Again, within the three stories, different moments from the character's past are edited so as to balance or contrast one with another. When Beckett was organising the multiple segments into a particular running order, in the manuscript he called what he was doing the 'Continuity'.[70] He might equally well have used the term 'montage'. For his own production of the play at the Schiller Theatre Werkstatt in Berlin in October 1976, Beckett also worked on the Listener's (minimal) reactions and on the short fades of light, which are carefully keyed to the opening and shutting of Listener's eyes.[71]

Play is a striking example of the success of fast inter-cutting, as the light shines rapidly first on one of the three heads, then on another, prompting each of them to speak in turn. In this play, Beckett combined multiple short individual and choral segments but also (particularly as he became involved himself with productions of his play) experimented with variations in speed of the delivery and the intensity of both light and sound.[72] Jeanne Antoine-Dunne has pointed out that a more basic parallel exists between this play and Eisenstein's writings on film.[73] In an early essay entitled 'An Unexpected Juncture', Eisenstein spoke of the equivalence of the sensory apprehension of light and sound. 'Eisenstein came to the conclusion', writes Antoine-Dunne, 'that sound and visual perceptions were identical in terms of

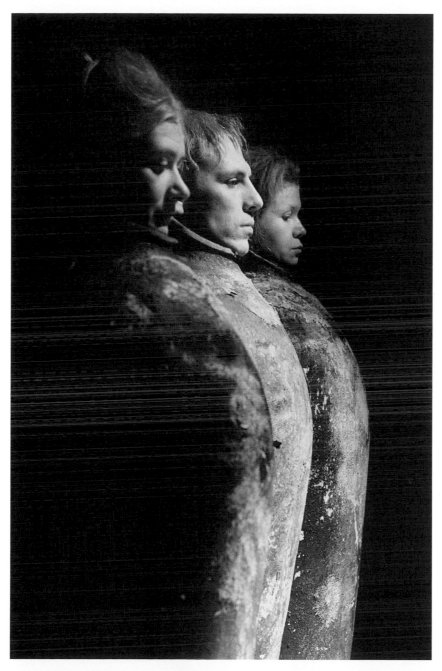

their effects on the nervous system because they both assail the body through a system of vibrations.'[74] And so, in Eisenstein's own words, 'while a shot is a visual perception and a tone is sound perception, both visual and sound overtones are totally physiological sensations'.[75] It seems to me that this common physiological attitude to sound and light lies behind both Beckett's harnessing of the two in *Play* and his insistence with *Not I* that it was 'addressed less to the understanding than to the nerves of the audience which should in a sense share her [that is Mouth's] bewilderment'; 'I hear it breathless, urgent, feverish, rhythmic, panting along, without undue concern with intelligibility', he wrote to Alan Schneider.[76]

Even *Endgame* and *Happy Days*, with stories delivered by Hamm and Winnie, contain major, repeated flashback sequences that are carefully cut into the main stage action. These sequences have frequently been written about as narratives woven into the fabric of the drama. What is less often pointed out is that Hamm, improvising his story, resembles the author of a scenario, modifying phrases here and there, always maintaining a strong emphasis on the visual as well as the verbal: 'The man came crawling towards me, on his belly. Pale, wonderfully pale and thin . . . I calmly filled my pipe – the *meerschaum*, lit it with . . . let us say a vesta, drew a few puffs . . . He raised his face to me,

Gillian Martell, Kenneth Cranham and Susan Williamson rehearsing *Play*, 1970

black with mingled dirt and tears.'[77] Winnie's tale of the Showers and Cookers who pass by and comment on her situation if less improvisational remains keenly visual. And the inter-cutting of the story as a memory that 'floats up' several times into her mind in both acts reminds one of a technique that is derived from film, even though the scene is dominated by the reported or imagined dialogue between Mr and Mrs Shower/Cooker – mediated, of course, through Winnie, the narrator.

Mime played a much more important part in Beckett's theatre than most critics have been willing to acknowledge. It is as if they were reluctant to concede that someone as determinedly intellectual as Beckett could possibly have been intrigued (and for so long) by something as apparently broad, simple and disingenuous as the slapstick humour of Keaton, Chaplin, Laurel and Hardy or the Marx Brothers. And yet he was. This prejudice also underestimates the complexity of thinking that lies behind mime and gesture. Mime, for instance, so often brings together the direct, the concrete and the indirect and ambiguous in a way that is characteristic of Beckett's own aesthetic. Some of the discussions of mime and gesture and their impact – by both Pudovkin and Arnheim, for example – were very analytical and very sophisticated.

Beckett wrote two wholly silent plays, *Act without Words* I and II, another pair of mimes, *Quad* I and II, which are played together and are almost dance pieces, a haunting mime for television, *Nacht und Träume*, which used the music of the Schubert *Lied* of that name, as well as two earlier discarded mimes, which he tried to write for Jack MacGowran and never managed to finish. In addition, smaller-scale mimes occur repeatedly in the major plays. In *Waiting for Godot*, Lucky's dance mime, 'The Net', is far from being the only instance of mime. Estragon enacts silently the taking off and putting on of his boots and, among other 'numbers', the two tramp-clowns reproduce the famous 'three hats for two heads' music hall set-piece. In act 1, Estragon mimics 'why he doesn't put down his bags?' while, in act 2, Vladimir mimes the actions of the tiger in his 'the tiger bounds' speech. In Beckett's own production, all the different elements of the mimes and the stage business – often involving objects like boots, hats, a basket, a stool, a whip, a pipe, a handkerchief and chicken bones – were developed and interrelated one with another.

Endgame and Krapp's Last Tape both open with extended silent or almost silent mimes that, as a director, Beckett spent lots of rehearsal time getting right. Happy Days even plays with the idea of mime by enacting an invisible one, the spectator being led to imagine what is happening as Winnie recounts how the (then unseen) Willie 'backs into' his hole in the ground. Several plays by Beckett include characters who do not themselves speak: the Buster Keaton figure O in Film; Joe in Eh Joe; the Auditor in Not I; the Listener in That Time; the male Figure in Ghost Trio; and the Protagonist in Catastrophe. Sometimes, as in Eh Joe and Krapp's Last Tape, Beckett plays on the expressiveness of the human face, as Joe listens to the woman's voice in his head, trying his best to throttle it, and as Krapp listens more or less silently but reacts visibly to his own younger voice on tape. More often he deliberately restricts or even totally excludes facial reactions to the words, as in That Time and Catastrophe. As Gontarski summarised: 'The sheer number of such works in which silence is person-ified, em-bodied, character-ized underscores the dominance of the visual in Samuel Beckett's theatre, and often as an element isolated and separated from the flow of words.'[78]

This emphasis on mime throughout Beckett's work almost certainly resulted from his long-standing interest in silent film. Arnheim wrote positively about its virtues, 'It was from its very silence that film received the impetus as well as the power to achieve excellent artistic effects.'[79] Beckett, too, was keenly aware of how powerful silence and stillness or near stillness could be. Indeed, one of the most striking parallels between Arnheim and Beckett revolves around this issue of stillness. In a subtle piece of analysis of the still photograph, Arnheim wrote that

a still photograph inserted in the middle of a moving film gives a very curious sensation; chiefly because the speed with which time is passing in the moving shots is carried over to the still picture, whose effect therefore is similar to that produced by holding one expression for an uncomfortably long time. And just as the time is carried over, so the rigidity is, as it were felt as movement, that is suspension of movement.[80]

When Beckett came to write his own film script for *Film*, he introduced seven still photographs, which are inspected one by one by the protagonist O. The effect is indeed 'curious' and for a number of different reasons: the rapid overview of a life replayed in these various frozen images; the varying lengths of time with which each photo is examined, depending on its subject; the delicate, almost affectionate touch of the forefinger on the face of a little girl, held in the arms of a man in uniform; the trembling of the hands as he holds what are clearly personally moving photos five and six. The fact that shots of the still photos also mostly include in the frame the head of O or his hands trying to tear up the photos inevitably raises questions in the mind of the spectator as to what the relationship is between O and those photographed (except for one) seemingly long ago. But the contrast between movement and suspension of movement certainly contributes to the effect of the scene. And although Arnheim distinguished between the 'absolute rigidity of a photograph' and the freezing of movement by an actor, it is quite possible that it was as a consequence of thinking about these questions that Beckett was prompted to lay as much store as he did in his theatre and his directing on still, frozen moments.[81] Arnheim's other section heading, the 'Artistic Utilisation of the Absence', is paradigmatic of Beckett's entire approach to theatre, in which the silence, the pause and the 'frozen tableau' are so vital to the impact of the drama, since, by being framed or highlighted, absence and the void are able to draw attention to themselves without the embarrassment of over statement.[82]

The gestures and movements of mime similarly stand out when they are not accompanied by words. Pantomime usually replaced the spoken word in the films of Chaplin and Keaton that Beckett so much admired. Arnheim spoke of 'the incredible visual concreteness of every one of his scenes' that was an important part of Chaplin's art.[83] And, again, Beckett had seen many times in films that he admired how powerfully expressive such mimes could be. When recounting the scene in D. W. Griffiths' 1916 film *Intolerance*, in which a woman hears the death sentence that has been passed on her husband, Pudovkin wrote in his book, *Film Technique*: 'The director shows the face of the woman: an anxious, trembling smile through

tears. Suddenly the spectator sees for an instant her hands, only her hands, the fingers compulsively gripping the skin. This is one of the most powerful moments in the film. Not for a minute did we see the whole figure, but only the face, and the hands.' Pudovkin drew some resonant conclusions from this scene: 'Here once more we encounter the process . . . of clear selection, the possibility of the elimination of those insignificances that fulfil only a transition function and are always inseparable from reality, and of the retention only of climactic and dramatic points.'[84]

It seems probable that the concentration on a few expressive gestures or movements, the tightness of focus and the emphasis on the concrete that Beckett brought to his late stage and television plays emanated at least in part from his own response to such powerful moments in silent films. Even the way that he isolated a part of the human body (the head or the mouth) at the expense of the whole figure may well represent a transposition from the use of close-up and selection in the cinema, as well as, it was suggested earlier, a theatrical development of the fragmentation and distortions that are found in some movements in modern art. Indeed, as we saw with painting, Beckett showed, throughout his career, an exceptional ability (and a readiness) to transfer ideas and techniques from one medium to another, ostensibly quite different one, rethinking

Patrick Magee in *That Time*, 1976

them, sometimes very radically, to test and stretch the boundaries of the new medium.

As a director, Beckett emphasised what, revealingly, he referred to many times as 'frozen tableaux'. In his production of *Waiting for Godot*, each act began with a lengthy (and newly introduced) '*wartestelle*' or 'waiting point' (with, contrary to the text, both Estragon and Vladimir present on stage, although separate). At these moments, the actors were frozen into immobility, sitting or standing in total silence. There were some twelve of these major extended waiting points throughout the play, most of which were not indicated in the published stage directions. At other times, too, in *Godot* and in many of his other plays, Beckett froze the action to allow a silent *tableau vivant* to impinge on the spectator. In a notebook prepared for his second production of *Endgame* with the San Quentin Drama Workshop at the Riverside Studios in London, he also used the term 'frozen postures' and, during the earlier production in Berlin, his assistant, Michael Haerdter, said of Beckett's work with the German actors that 'over and over, he has them freeze for seconds at a time into a tableau which is to achieve its effect through repetition'.[85]

Beckett's various productions of *Krapp's Last Tape* similarly included a whole set of different 'frozen postures'. At the beginning and then again at the very end of the play, Krapp sat transfixed, like a figure captured on canvas in a painting, with his hands outstretched on the table in front of him. There was a second 'listening' posture, during which, as Krapp listened to passages from a tape recording of his voice made thirty years ago, with his hand poised on the on–off switch of the tape recorder, his movements were minimal. A third, quite different frozen tableau was the 'brooding' or 'dream' position, during which Krapp held his head up in the air, turned slightly to the right, as if mesmerised, a posture which he adopted at all those points on the tape when his recorded voice invoked sensual memories of the various women who had played a part in his life.

In Beckett's own two productions, *Happy Days* started from just such another frozen position, which Beckett described as Winnie's 'sleeping pose'. Imprisoned in her mound of earth, with her head down on her arms and curled up in sleep, Winnie stirred only after several piercing bursts of the alarm bell had awakened her to live through 'another heavenly day'. Her busy movements evolved from yet another static posture in which her arms rested on the ground, with fingertips just touching. She reverted to this position throughout the play, as she urged herself to go 'on Winnie'. She also halted facing the front whenever 'words fail' and 'sorrow keeps breaking in', or, again paused, often holding objects in her hands, as she dredged up a quotation from an increasingly failing memory bank of 'classics' or as she evoked a memory from the remote past. Beckett encouraged the actress at these points to adopt a whole series of related positions for her head, her torso and her arms, which echoed across entire passages of text in the first act. In the second act, when Winnie is buried up to her neck, gestures are of course no longer possible, yet a few minimal movements of her head, and above all her eyes and eyebrows, remain to animate this 'talking head' that again reverts quite naturally to a number of set positions.

The effects of such 'frozen tableaux' and 'frozen postures' in Beckett's plays were varied and complex. They allowed the spectator time to scrutinise the scene in a way that is more commonly associated with the attention accorded to the visual imagery of a painting. There we dwell at length or move at will from one part of the picture to another, yet at the same time we are affected by the entire picture. But Beckett knew perfectly well that a flesh-and-blood actor is not, and never can be, a wholly static or still-life image, although at times he might be made to resemble one: in even the stillest of postures, eyes blink, lips quiver, hands tremble. And, in *Krapp's Last Tape*, the emphasis on frozen postures meant that, when Krapp did react to what he heard, his movements, gestures and facial expressions registered more sharply as a consequence. The same applied to Winnie's increasingly limited range of expressive possibilities.

This 'more means less' principle was one that Beckett followed quite consistently in his directing. The tiniest of movements seemed as a result larger and more compelling than they actually were: with Krapp, the drop of a head, a sharp or puzzled look at the tape recorder, a movement of his hand to his brow to wipe the dream away; with Winnie, the look and the facial expressions and tiny movements of face and eyes that accompany it; the closing of the eyes and the enigmatic smile at the end of *That Time*. The frozen moments also enabled Beckett to confer visual shape on his play, a shape that provided it with clear divisions between immobility and movement and silence and speech, and yet they also allowed subtle interaction between these differing sets of oppositions.

While Beckett was directing *Footfalls* at the Royal Court Theatre in London, he said to Rose Hill, who was playing the part of Mother: 'We are not doing this play realistically or psychologically, we are doing it musically.' This remark could be applied to all his productions. They were dominated by an idea that he had expressed in the early 1960s when he said: 'producers [i.e. directors] don't seem to have any sense of form in movement, the kind of form one finds in music, for instance, where themes keep recurring. When, in a text, actions are repeated, they ought to be made unusual the first time, so that when they happen again – in exactly the same way – an audience will recognise them from before.'[86]

Beckett was not by any means the first dramatist to handle themes musically in his writing nor, even less, the first director to apply musical techniques to his work. But he was exceptional in the lengths to which he was prepared to carry it. Rarely has anyone orchestrated a 'score' quite so minutely so as to include gestures and movements as well as words and sounds. The result was that all these different elements became integrated into a complex network of *interrelated* musical or choreographic echoes.

Beckett had been an accomplished, if amateur, pianist since his early youth and was married to Suzanne Descheveaux-Dumesnil, a pianist who had trained at the Ecole Normale de Musique and was a more talented performer than he was. He was a fervent admirer of the music of Schubert, Beethoven and Haydn, but he also played a wide repertoire of piano music: Chopin, Mozart, Debussy and Bartók, among others.[87] He loved going to concerts in Paris. At home or with his friends, Avigdor and Anne Arikha, he regularly used to listen to France Musique concerts on the radio or play gramophone

records of classical music. He and Suzanne were also close friends of the Romanian-French composer, Marcel Mihalovici, and his concert pianist wife, Monique Haas, whose recitals they often used to attend. It should come as no surprise, then, to discover that he harnessed his easy familiarity with music and with musical forms to the direction of his plays.

With the musically trained Rose Hill, and, earlier, with the German cast of *Endgame*, Beckett used quite naturally terms like 'scherzo', 'legato', 'andante' or 'piano'. In Berlin, he commented to the actors that there were 'still many false notes' and 'still no rhythm'.[88] He described *Happy Days* to Billie Whitelaw as a 'sonata for voice and movement' and told her that *Rockaby* should have 'the quality of a lullaby'.[89] And, in his production notebooks he invoked the occasional musical analogy. For example, in his *Krapp's Last Tape* notebook he described the vocal principle that he had in mind as a slide from the major key (expressing a tone of assurance) into the minor key (which betrayed its artificiality), whenever three themes appeared in the play to disrupt the initial tone: solitude, light and darkness and Woman.

It is not just that Beckett used the vocabulary of music in his notebooks or at rehearsals with those actors who understood his musical terminology. As a writer he paid close and persistent attention to repetition and repetition with variation, echo,

Rose Hill and Leslie Sarony in *Endgame*, 1976

rhythm and balance. As a director, he worked hard to introduce further echoes and intricate parallels into his plays.

On occasion, he was even prepared to change the words of his original text and the stage directions in order to create additional verbal or visual patterns, which echoed from one section of the play to another. For example, in the 1984 English production of *Waiting for Godot* with the San Quentin Drama Workshop, on which he collaborated with his former assistant, Walter Asmus, he altered many of Estragon's responses to Vladimir's reiterated 'We're waiting for Godot.' The replies, which had varied in the printed text between 'Fancy that', 'True' and 'Good idea', were transformed in the San Quentin production into the identical 'Ah yes' – a choice influenced by his liking for the German, '*Ach ja*' – which, through constant repetition, assumed an additional burden of lassitude every time it was uttered. At the very end of the play, when Vladimir told Estragon to pull on his trousers, instead of saying, as he did in the published English text, 'True', Estragon replied again, 'Ah yes', finishing with the laugh line that Beckett wanted – but a laugh line that, because of its association with the 'We're waiting for Godot' line that it had so often followed, had also acquired melancholic associations.

In revising his English text for the San Quentin production, Beckett also restored several passages of dialogue partly to bring the text more closely in line with the French original, but also to develop and extend the verbal echoes. One intriguing addition (which he had already made in German in his Schiller Theatre production) related to the question as to whether Mr Godot's beard was 'fair or black'. To this, Beckett added the colour 'or red?' This linked Godot with the earlier brothel story of whether the client wanted a blonde, a brunette or a redhead. It was characteristic of Beckett that the momentous – Godot on whom all their hopes appeared to rest – should have been linked by analogy to the trivial or, in this case, the scatological.

In *Happy Days*, when Winnie took a strand of her hair from under her hat, by a slight change of text, Beckett created one of the simplest, yet most moving moments of the play. She no longer let the strand of hair fall – as she did in the printed text – but continued to hold it in her left hand, as she said nostalgically: 'Golden you called it, that day, the last guest gone (*hand up in gesture raising a glass*) to your golden . . . may it never (*voice breaks*) . . . may it never . . . That day. . . . What day?'[90] But in this case both the gestures and the text ('when the last guest was gone' has been shortened to 'the last guest gone') were changed in Beckett's productions, so that when, in the second act, Winnie said 'That day. The pink fizz. The flute glasses. The last guest gone',[91] we could recall with remembered emotion the earlier gestures and words that echoed movingly across a large stretch of the play.

The echoes and patterns were not only verbal. They applied to movements, gestures and sounds. In one of his theatre notebooks prepared for the Schiller Theatre production of *Waiting for Godot*, Beckett wrote 'establish at [the] outset 2 caged dynamics, E. [Estragon] sluggish, V. [Vladimir] restless + perpetual separation and reunion of V/E.'[92] So Vladimir moved restlessly towards and away from Estragon, who, except very occasionally, either stayed seated or moved as little and as lethargically as possible. The pattern of these moves often followed what Beckett called an 'approach by stages', so that one of the tramps would advance towards the other in a series of short stops and starts, often patterned in rhythmic groups of three.

These moves formed an important part of the stage dynamics, lending vitality to what might otherwise have been a somewhat static scene. But they also introduced visual motifs and precise patterns that echoed from one moment of the play to another. Beckett called such repetitions 'themes of the body'. When Vladimir felt lonely, for example, while Estragon was sleeping, and approached his friend in a number of stages (a 'step-by-step approach' Beckett called it), wakening him with his cries of 'Gogo! . . . Gogo! . . . Gogo!', he was directly paralleling Estragon's earlier 'calendar stops' as he had asked 'But what Saturday? And is it Saturday? / Is it not rather Sunday? Or Monday? / Or Friday?'[93] While Estragon was sleeping, Vladimir did not, as in the published text, 'pace agitatedly to and fro'; instead, in Beckett's production, he followed – but in an anti-clockwise direction – the exact route that Estragon had taken earlier in a clockwise direction, as he inspected the spot at which they found themselves waiting for Godot. The same route was

then mirrored by Vladimir at the opening of the second act. All of these visual echoes became physical parallels involving both of the tramps/friends and, in their turn, they mirrored the verbal patterns that recurred repeatedly throughout the play.

In Beckett's Schiller Theatre production of *Endgame*, Clov's footsteps back and forth from the kitchen to Hamm's chair were of a consistent number and pattern and were always rhythmically timed: 'It's almost like a dance', says Beckett, 'equal number of steps, rhythm kept equal.'[94] He normally had a well-thought-out intellectual rationale behind everything that he did, and, in this case, this may have been provided by his readings in the 1930s in the history of Greek philosophy, which would have supplied him with an additional motivation for his emphasis on repetition and pattern. At rehearsals in Berlin, after organising Clov's steps from his kitchen to Hamm's armchair, Beckett referred to the repeated numbers as being 'Pythagorean'. Clearly what he had in mind was Pythagoras' theory in which the universe consisted of a harmonious disposition of numbers, based on the perfect number 10. Again, using such repeated patterns as a unifying feature, Beckett organised Clov's short steps when he is 'having an idea' into a series of $6 + 4 + 6 + 4$.[95]

Beckett also put together rhythmical patterns of action and sound, one often interrelating with the other. In the printed text of *Waiting for Godot*, Vladimir first takes off his bowler hat, feels about inside it, shakes it, then twice knocks on the crown 'as though to dislodge a foreign body'.[96] Estragon then takes off his boot and similarly 'feels about inside it, turns it upside down and shakes it'.[97] In the San Quentin production this is how the action went: Vladimir took off his hat, shook it as before, knocked twice (knock, knock) on the crown. Estragon then took off his boot, felt inside it, shook it but then gave an exactly answering knock (knock, knock) on the sole of the boot. A few lines later, Vladimir once again took off his hat, went through the same routine once again, giving the same answering knocks (again two) in the same rhythm as Estragon's on the boot. This involved only minor

(*Left*) Barry McGovern and Johnny Murphy in *Waiting for Godot*, 1999

changes to the stage directions but a rhythmical sound patterning was introduced that was analogous to the visual patterning. The (quite busy) stage business was structured in this way into a pleasing choreography that involved both gestures and sounds.

In his productions of *Endgame*, Nagg's knocks on Nell's dustbin were made to echo the knocks that Hamm made on the 'hollow wall'. Once again the repetition principle meant that the sound patterns sometimes provided auditory echoes with the verbal text. Only occasionally did Beckett have second thoughts about such echoes, when he feared that he might be drawing too much attention to them, making the parallels too explicit. One such hesitation was when he changed the text so that Hamm called Clov at the end of the play (in the German production but not the London one) not once (as in the printed texts) but twice, to echo Nagg's earlier 'Nell . . . Nell' and Hamm's call of 'Father . . . Father'.[98]

In *Krapp's Last Tape* even the non-verbal sounds that Krapp uttered and the noises that he made with objects were all orchestrated by Beckett into a kind of musical score complementary to the verbal text. This sonic score included: the shuffle of Krapp's shoes on the wooden stage during the banana business and his fast, squeaky footsteps as he walked excitedly to and from his den; his hand banging noisily down on the table; his strangulated cries or laughs, even his heavy breathing and his grunts; the sounds of a bottle chinking against the glass; noises made while he was drinking. Krapp's voice itself used musical pitch in a varied and interesting way: the deep bass of the older Krapp; the lighter tones of the 39-year-old; the high, almost falsetto note that he adopted for the repeated word 'Spool'.

'As much noise as poss. with objects throughout', wrote Beckett in his director's notebook for the Berlin production of *Krapp's Last Tape*.[99] And his concern for the patterning of sounds affected even his choice of props. The cardboard boxes of the original texts became tin boxes in order to clatter as they were set down on the table, or as they fell on the floor; the dictionary was to be 'enormous', again so that it would make a loud bang as it was dropped on the table; the drawer was to run freely so that it shut with a loud 'explosion' of sound. These various sounds were organised rhythmically, as one might

orchestrate the percussion parts of an orchestral score. Sharp sounds punctuated the silence, just as sudden movements broke up the stillness. Discussing the sounds that Krapp might make with his mouth, Beckett wrote in his notes: 'With the silence (immobility) of the listening phase these form a balance in terms of sound with the duo immobility agitation.'[100] But again, as deviations from their opposites, they also threw those opposites into greater prominence. So the silence appeared deeper precisely because of the sharpness and the intensity of the sounds that broke into it, and the sounds were similarly highlighted because of the silences from which they sprang.

One of the most interesting aspects of Beckett's directing was that he organised gestures just as musically and just as precisely as he did the text or the movements. Few directors have carried musical principles as far into this area. In *Happy Days*, for instance, Winnie frequently reached into her bag to take out an object – her mirror, toothbrush, magnifying glass, lipstick, even a gun. In Beckett's productions, all her movements were orchestrated into an intricate choreography of repeated actions, what Peter Hall aptly called 'a precise ballet of ordinariness'.[101] 'You peer in, see what things are there and get them out. Peer, take, place; peer, take, place', 'what a precise manipulator she is', he said to Billie Whitelaw, who played Winnie.[102] In this way, a structure of recurring movements was established that echoed

Leslie Sarony and Stephen Rea in *Endgame*, 1976

Billie Whitelaw in *Happy Days*, 1979

the repeated 'notes' of the text but also contributed to its own 'subliminal imagery' (Beckett's phrase).

What is clear is that the author-director was deliberately adopting repeated patterns of moves, actions, gestures and sounds so that they would gradually infiltrate themselves into the unconscious of the spectator. Indeed, he described the process as being like 'the effect of those recurring images inserted into films for propaganda purposes which penetrate the subconscious by repetition'.[103]

Beckett's concern for balance, rhythm and contrast led him when he was directing to discover, explore and then develop patterns or echoes that were often deeply embedded within his text. He seized on what might appear at first to be disparate elements and linked them together. These links could be close or they could be quite remote. Sometimes they functioned at a phonic or a gestural level only: lines distant from each other were linked because they might possess the same number of syllables or similar sounding cadences; apparently unrelated gestures were brought together to form an echoing pattern. For example, Krapp will, Beckett wrote in his notebook, employ the same 'way of closing [the dictionary] on "Witwenvogel" [the vidua-bird]' 'as that of the ledger on "Liebe" [love]'.[104] This was the visual equivalent of pronouncing certain phrases in the same tone as others. Just as Krapp adopted the same 'dream' posture and look every time an encounter with a woman was alluded to, so the voice on the tape employed what Beckett described as 'Ton fille [Woman tone]' at these points in the text.[105] 'Same reaction as' was to become one of the most common of notes in his production notebook.

Yet, as the last example suggests, Beckett's work as a director was not purely formal and certainly not incidental or decorative. Repetition, balance and contrast are not, then, merely structural devices, but are closely related to fundamental thematic concerns that are woven poetically into the plays.

During rehearsals of *Waiting for Godot*, Beckett said pointedly of Lucky's monologue, 'It is all about stones, about the world of stones' and Walter Asmus quoted the author-director's remarks that 'Estragon is on the ground, he belongs to the stone. Vladimir is light, he is oriented towards the sky. He belongs to the tree.'[106] In the context of such a vision of the world, the two central figures were linked by Beckett's directorial choices with what might be called an elemental or cosmological set of contrasts: earth–sky; mineral–vegetable; material–immaterial; horizontal–vertical; aspiration up and impulsion down. Once again, he made changes to the script, replacing the 'low mound' of the published texts with a 'stone' in the opening stage directions. He also later altered his text when the tramps seek to identify the place at which they are to meet Mr Godot: 'That tree . . . that stone . . . that bog', Beckett adding 'that stone'.[107] He then had Estragon return to sit on the stone or stand close to it far more often than in the printed text. On the few occasions when Estragon and Vladimir were at the stone together, the former left little space for Vladimir to sit down. Vladimir never sat there alone. By contrast, Vladimir's basic orientation was, as Beckett suggested, to the tree and the sky. So, directing the play, he increased the number of Vladimir's movements in the direction of the tree and the frequency with which he gazed at the sky.

Some of the ways in which Beckett approached *Waiting for Godot* as a director were even subtler than this and were clearly intended to operate on the hidden, 'subliminal' level of which he had spoken. The dominant pattern of the moves that Estragon and Vladimir followed, for example, in both the Schiller and the San Quentin productions consisted mainly of semi-circles, arcs and chords. This aptly reflected the closed, circular universe in which his characters existed. Moreover, when they did move in straight lines, they appeared to be tracing out hidden cruciform patterns along the upstage horizontal line and back down the vertical centre line on the raked stage of the Schiller Theatre in Berlin, echoing (again subliminally) the crucifixion imagery that runs through the entire play. Estragon and Vladimir sometimes stood one on either side of the tree, reflecting the tree/cross (with an absent Christ) surrounded by the two thieves.

In discussing Estragon's and Vladimir's movements, Beckett wrote in his notes for the Schiller Theatre production that the 'general effect of moves especially V's [Vladimir's] though apparently motivated that of those in a

cage'.[108] At one moment he even considered having the 'faint shadow of bars on the stage floor',[109] in the end deciding that this was much too explicit. Beckett's characters were, as Lucky's dance suggested, imprisoned in a net, able to move only along the strands of its mesh. Their movements to and fro resembled, then, those of the caged owls, bears and apes that appear in his early poems and prose. When, in the Schiller Theatre production, the two friends go offstage during Lucky's 'think', they merely beat their wings like trapped birds, bouncing back, as if on elastic, into the stage space to which they are inextricably confined.

The theme of imprisonment is one that pervades almost the whole of Beckett's theatre. In *Godot*, Estragon and Vladimir are (whatever they say) 'tied' to Godot. Pozzo and Lucky are, literally and metaphorically, linked one to the other by the rope. In *Endgame*, Nagg and Nell are physically imprisoned in their dustbins, just as Hamm is confined to his wheelchair. Hamm and Clov are also both mentally tied to the room. The figures in *Play* are stuck in funeral urns, immured in a strange kind of limbo, each of them a victim of the interrogating beam of light. As a director, Beckett underlined this aspect of his writing while again seeking not to make it too explicit. He wrote, for instance, to Rick Cluchey when he was about to play Krapp in Berlin under his direction that 'he should make the thing his own in terms of incarceration, for example. Incarceration in self.'

Greg Hicks and Denis Quilley in *Waiting for Godot*, 1997

He escapes from the trap of the other, only to be trapped in self.'[110] He told Hildegard Schmahl when they were rehearsing *Footfalls* together that as May she was 'totally encapsulated within herself'.[111] Seen through the filter of Beckett's own productions, Lucky's dance, 'The Net', expresses in a dramatically arresting way a much wider view of man as a prisoner of life, imprisoned either in dependence or in loneliness. It was a chilling view of human existence but it was authentic and it was deeply felt.

Happy Days is built on stark contrasts and, in directing it on two separate occasions, Beckett picked up the conflicting impulses that run through it. The most striking of these is between Winnie's 'look on the bright side' philosophy with her repeated phrases of reassurance ('great mercies', 'That is what I find so wonderful', etc.) and the harsh realities of her dreadful predicament. But there are other important, related contrasts. Beckett touched on the elemental clashes in Winnie's world with the actress Eva-Katarina Schultz, when he told her: 'She is a weightless being, being devoured by a cruel earth.'[112] Winnie's natural element is the air and she aspires to escape, 'simply float up into the blue . . . like gossamer'. After the parasol bursts into flames in the heat of the sun, she asks herself: 'Shall I myself not melt perhaps in the end, or burn, oh I do not mean necessarily burst into flames. No just little by little be charred to a black cinder, all this – (*ample gesture of arms*) – visible flesh.'[113] Yet she sinks or is sucked down into the 'earth you old extinguisher'. As we saw earlier, Beckett had done a lot of reading of Greek philosophy in the 1930s and was familiar with the different theories propounded on the nature of the universe, including that of Heraclitus of Ephesus. In his philosophical notes, Beckett had written about the 'double process' that existed in Heraclitus' thinking: 'Upward convergence of all things to fire and life, downward divergence of all things from fire and water, earth and death.'[114] Such ideas clearly lurk behind the images of fire and earth in *Happy Days*, but, equally clearly, they are there for their dramatic value, and not for their 'truth value' – as Beckett himself said about his use of Bishop Berkeley's ideas on perception in *Film*.

In Beckett's own productions, the contrast between aspiration upwards and movement downwards operated at both a literal and a metaphorical level

and informed both Winnie's busy chatter and her most ordinary gestures. Often the would-be cheerfulness of her first-act voice was pierced by darker tones, as sorrow repeatedly 'keeps breaking in'. The second act was consistently dark and contrasted with the lighter tones of the first act. In Beckett's production notebook, he registered some of these contrasts by noting them with plus and minus signs. He even annotated Winnie's very first words, specifically remarking on their 'dualism', recording them as 'Another (−) heavenly day (+)'.[115] These contrasts between lightness and heaviness, optimism and sorrow, expansion and contraction, were also echoed in Winnie's movements. So her gesture as she went to pray was halted and her swooping movements when she reached into her bag were arrested, as she confronted the danger of running out of things to do or to say.

In the *Happy Days* notebooks, a number of other major themes were introduced or implied. One such theme emerged as Beckett outlined how the primary elements of the objects that Winnie used had wasted away, while their secondary elements had developed abnormally. He expressed this most succinctly in the notes that he made for the 1979 Royal Court Theatre production as 'Gen. [i.e. general] principle: hypertrophy secondary atrophy primary'.[116] But, in notes prepared for his Schiller Theatre production eight years before, he elaborated on this theme and widened it

Billie Whitelaw in *Happy Days*, 1979

considerably, writing, 'Conspicuousness. Inadequacy or exiguity of primary element (brush, glass), as compared with secondary (handle, etc.). Narrowness and elongation. Agedness. Endingness.'[117] The parasol with which Winnie seeks to protect herself from the fierce heat of the sun has, then, a long handle, but too small a canopy to do this. For although 'things have their life', they constantly intrude upon the comfort and bearable nature of Winnie's existence. Objects and persons participate in a world that is characterised by displacement, disunity, fragmentation and disarray.

Probably the closest Beckett came to discussing crucial themes of his play with an actor or actress was with Eva-Katarina Schultz, who played Winnie in the Schiller Theatre production of *Happy Days*. Winnie, he explained briefly to the actress, could not understand time because she felt she existed in a present without end and because the past could have no possible meaning for her.[118] In his notebook, he wrote expansively: 'her time experience, incomprehensible transport from one inextricable present to the next, those past unremembered, those to come inconceivable'.[119] Winnie's puzzled statement, 'Then . . . now . . . what difficulties here, for the mind. (*Pause*.) To have been always what I am – and so changed from what I was. (*Pause*.) I am the one. I say the one, then the other'[120] applied just as much to present as it did to past time. In Beckett's productions this experience of time was reflected in Winnie's volatility of mood as well as in the fragmentation of her thought, her speech and her movements.

The slow, inexorable yet unending 'grain upon grain' theme of time dominated both Beckett's 1967 Schiller Theatre and 1980 San Quentin productions of *Endgame*. 'Finished, it's finished, nearly finished, it must be nearly finished',[121] announced Clov at the beginning of the play. And Beckett's production notes focused on the way in which this theme was articulated throughout the play. He structured stage time very precisely by a combination of Clov's refrain, 'I'll leave you', repeated ten times and at regular intervals, and of Hamm's question, 'is it not time for my pain-killer?' reiterated six times, again at regular intervals. In Beckett's productions, the 'running out' process did not proceed regularly, but occurred in minute grains with deadly slowness. His San Quentin notebook suggests indeed that

Beckett saw one of these changes as having happened before the play began. His note on the beginning of the play reads: 'C [Clov] perplexed. All seemingly in order, yet a change. Fatal grain added to form impossible heap. *Ratio ruentis acervi*. Last straw.'[122] Within a matter of moments from the opening of the play, Hamm and Nagg are told that there are no more bicycle wheels, no more pap, no more nature. Yet – in the English text – it is another twenty-five pages before Clov announces in, for this play, rapid succession that there are no more tides, navigators, rugs, painkillers and coffins. So, another grain appears to have been added to the pile, although, since the informant is Clov, we cannot be absolutely certain that he is telling the truth.

One of the most important changes that Beckett made in the 1980 San Quentin production was to add further levels of deliberate deceitfulness to Clov's relations with Hamm. This deceit emanated from Clov's desire to move about the refuge as little as possible, because his movements were so painful. Clov was, wrote Beckett in the San Quentin notes, 'stiff, gone at knees/waist. When still tries to straighten, restoops . . . moving painful as economical as possible.'[123] As a consequence, instead of moving to the back wall after 'Then move' and instead of climbing up the ladder first to open and then to close the window, he stayed (in Beckett's note) '*sur place*' (on the spot), pretending to walk by performing a brief tramp-tramp on the stage (two steps loud, two steps less loud), or again pretending to climb the steps by knocking on them. This was echoed by the crescendo of thumps that Beckett suggested Clov should give to Hamm's chair, instead of moving it, when the tyrant wanted it put 'Bang in the centre'. 'It's a lie! Why do you lie to me?', Hamm had just asked.[124] And as Hamm went on bullying, so Clov went on deceiving. In these ways, Beckett's directing clarified the cruelly symbiotic relationship that lies at the hub of his play and translated the major theme of the 'difficulty of ending' into the minutiae of acting detail.

In what is by far the clearest illustration of how closely Beckett's directing methods are related to his thematic concerns, in his *Krapp's Last Tape* notes he identified and explored the Gnostic or Manichean oppositions that make up the intellectual infrastructure of the play.[125] Later, he claimed that his analysis derived from viewing the play more objectively from the outside in order to direct it. However, looking at the evolution of the play's manuscripts, it is difficult to believe that he was not already fully aware of the dualistic divisions, which were an essential part of Gnostic thinking, while he was writing or (at the very least) while he was revising it. And to anyone who knows the play at all well, it is impossible to accept that the analytical remarks in the notebook were the 'ravings', that, either self-deprecatingly or self-defensively, he once described them as to me.[126] In fact, writing to Alan Schneider about the play in advance of the New York production, and years before he directed it himself, he revealed how crucial these contrasts seemed to him.

> With regard to costume it should be sufficiently clear from text (don't be afraid of exaggerating with boots). Black and white (both dirty), the whole piece being built up in one sense on this simple antithesis of which you will find echoes throughout the text (black ball, white nurse, black pram, Bianca, Kedar – anagram of 'dark' – Street, black storm, light of understanding, etc.) Black dictionary if you can and ledger. Similarly black and white set.[127]

Rudolf Arnheim in his book on film had already drawn attention to how effective such contrasting imagery was in Josef von Sternberg's 1928 silent film, *The Docks of New York*. He wrote that 'the primitive but always effective symbolism of Light *versus* Darkness, white purity *versus* black evil, the opposition between gloom and radiance, is inexhaustible. In Sternberg's "The Docks of New York", for example, the two chief characters in the film are characterised in this way. The pale face, the white dress, the light hair of the girl are in optical contrast to the black figure of the ship's stoker.'[128]

The Gnostic oppositions of light and darkness (identified in Beckett's notes as 'light and dark emblems' and mentioned sometimes as separate, sometimes as integrated) were incorporated in Beckett's productions into the set, stage props and Krapp's costume. Moreover, he added other light and dark elements additional to those already present in the published texts: the den at the back of the stage was lit by a white light and was separated from the stage by a black curtain; the tin boxes, white envelope and dark wooden table picked up even more of these light and dark oppositions; the ledger

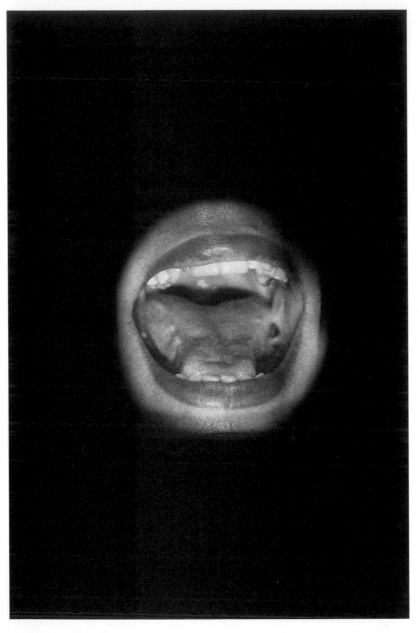

Niamh Cusack in *Not I*, 1999

consulted by Krapp was large, worn and black in colour, while Beckett wanted the dictionary to be bound in a light-coloured leather. Many of Krapp's actions and movements were again determined to some extent by Gnostic divisions. In the preliminary action, Krapp stepped into the darkness surrounding the table before returning to his zone of light and threw the banana skins and remaining piece of banana into the darkness. During the play, he looked slowly around him (looking for death, with whom he shortly has an unscheduled appointment) on three separate occasions and walked through the dark on his way to the second area of light in his cubby-hole. Directing the play, Beckett chose, then, to highlight the external manifestations of the divisions that lie at its thematic centre.

With repetition above all perhaps, Beckett's most frequently used device, 'structure and meaning blend into one another'.[129] To take only one example, repetition lies, for instance, at the very heart of *Krapp's Last Tape*. With both his 'listening to an old year, passages at random' and his birthday recording, Krapp repeats a ceremony that he has been performing for the past forty-five years. The many repetitions and echoes link Krapp with his former self, and yet allow us to perceive discontinuity as well – to hear some of the same ideas and phrases, and yet to note the change of voice and tone and see his decline from assurance to slightly bitter resignation mixed with nostalgic

yearning. The repetition of the tape with the girl in the punt fascinates Krapp but also leads him inexorably back to that sense of loss and failure in which the play is steeped. Looking at the play from the outside (in as much as he could do so) in order to direct it brought Beckett to focus on themes that widened the resonance of his work and to incorporate details into his directing that removed what was inessential and highlighted the central theme of separation or reconciliation.

Early in his career as a writer, Beckett recognised the fundamental importance of silence in music. In his letter written in German in 1937 to Axel Kaun, he suggested that it should be possible to dissolve 'the terrible materiality of the word surface . . . like for example the sound surface, torn by enormous pauses, of Beethoven's seventh symphony'.[130] In writing plays, such a possibility became a concrete reality for Beckett. Silence held both positive and negative associations in his theatre. It allowed him to capture 'a whisper of that final music or that silence that underlies all', while it retained at the same time a strongly positive dramatic force.[131] This is particularly striking in *Waiting for Godot*, in which (in Beckett's own words) 'silence is pouring into this play like water into a sinking ship' and yet in which frozen moments of total silence compellingly hold our attention.[132] In *Krapp's Last Tape*, too, the associations between

Barry McGovern in *Waiting for Godot*, 1999

(*Right*) Samuel Beckett, directing *Happy Days* in 1979

silence, death and nothingness register infallibly, as silence evokes the non-being that lies in wait for Krapp. Yet it does this in the context of presence. Paradoxically, Krapp is never more dramatically real than when he freezes in total silence.

Sound and silence, immobility and movement all participate in a dynamic theatre of ambiguity, fragility and inexplicability. Beckett's comment on the 'subliminal' impact of his patterns and his echoes points to the subtlety and the delicacy of his art. As a director of his own plays, he naturally wanted to be as true as he possibly could to his vision, while creating aesthetically satisfying patterns of shapes, movements and sounds. But he also wanted to ensure that his visual as well as his verbal imagery would echo memorably in the mind of the spectator. Reference was anathema to him and both as a director and as a writer he worked through suggestion rather than explicit statement. It is evidence of his remarkable success that, so long after his death, memories of his productions remain so vividly etched in one's mind.

Notes

A PORTRAIT OF BECKETT

1 Samuel Beckett [in future notes referring to diary entries and letters, SB], unpublished German Diaries, vol. 2, 6 November 1936.

2 SB, German Diaries, vol. 3, 31 December 1936.

3 SB, letter to Ethna MacCarthy, 10 January 1959.

4 SB, letter to Jocelyn Herbert, 12 June 1972.

5 SB, letter to Mary Hutchinson, 24 August 1972.

6 SB, letter to Ruby Cohn, 6 February 1977.

7 SB, letter to Mary Hutchinson, 6 February 1977.

8 SB, letter to Jocelyn Herbert, 15 May 1977.

9 SB, letter to Larry Shainberg, 7 January 1983.

10 SB, letter to James Knowlson, 20 May 1981.

11 SB, letter to Jocelyn Herbert, 11 January 1981.

12 Samuel Beckett, *Proust and Three Dialogues with Georges Duthuit* (London: Calder & Boyars, 1970), p. 11. Beckett wrote these words in the 1931 first edition of *Proust*.

13 For example, Murphy in Beckett's novel of that name plays a game of chess against Mr Endon and *Endgame*, the title of which itself derives from chess terminology, also has elements that it shares with the game, for example, Hamm's opening 'Me to play.'

14 In Patrick Bowles, 'How to Fail', *PN Review* 96, vol. 20, no. 4, March–April 1994, p. 20, Bowles quotes Beckett as saying 'Hölderlin ended in something of this kind of failure. His only successes are the points where his poems go on, falter, stammer and then admit failure, and are abandoned. At such points he was most successful. When he tried to abandon the spurious magnificence.' Beckett was particularly fond of Hölderlin's 'Der Spaziergang' and 'Die Titanen'.

15 Samuel Beckett, undated conversation with James Knowlson at dinner in the PLM hôtel, boulevard Saint-Jacques, Paris.

16 Anne Atik, *How It Was. A Memoir of Samuel Beckett* (London: Faber & Faber, 2001).

17 Atik also spoke of how much Beckett admired Heine's poetry, ibid., p. 67.

18 Samuel Beckett, conversation with James Knowlson, 13 April 1983.

19 Bowles, 'How to Fail', p. 17.

20 All of these quotations are taken from Lawrence Harvey's notes on his conversations with Beckett on 7 November 1961, 22 February 1962 and 19 March 1962. The notes are preserved at Dartmouth College, New Hampshire.

21 These extensive notes made by Beckett in the early 1930s on his readings of histories of philosophy are now at Trinity College, Dublin, with copies in the archive of the Beckett International Foundation at the University of Reading.

22 See Atik, *How It Was*, pp. 7–11.

23 SB, letter to Tom MacGreevy, 18 January 1937.

24 SB, letter to James Knowlson, 28 October 1976.

25 SB, letter to Tom Bishop, 20 March 1973.

26 MS 2901, archive of the Beckett International Foundation, University of Reading.

27 In 1931 Beckett wrote to Tom MacGreevy: 'I read two books of Powys: *Mark Only* and *Mr Tasker's Gods* not knowing his work at all, and was very disappointed. Such a fabricated darkness and painfully organised unified tragic completeness. The Hardy sin caricatured.' SB, letter to Tom MacGreevy, 8 November 1931.

28 See also Alain Badiou's interesting discussion of this and other positive features of Beckett's writing in his book, *Beckett. L'increvable désir* (Paris: Hachette, 1995).

29 Nancy Cunard described Beckett in 1956 as looking 'like a magnificent Mexican sculpture now'. Anne Chisholm, *Nancy Cunard* (Harmondsworth: Penguin, 1981), p. 400.

30 SB, letter to Alan Schneider, 15 July 1967.

31 SB, letter to Nick Rawson, 1 March 1970.

32 SB, letter to Jocelyn Herbert, 3 October 1966.

33 SB, letter to Judith Schmidt, 27 April 1965.

34 Samuel Beckett, 'Draff' in *More Pricks than Kicks* (1st edition, London: Chatto & Windus, 1934; London: Calder & Boyars, 1970), p. 204. The quotation is used twice in *Dream of Fair to Middling Women* and also in *Watt*.

35 SB, letter to Pamela Mitchell, 25 November 1953.

36 SB, letter to John Kobler, 21 March 1977.

37 SB, letter to Tom MacGreevy, 10 March 1935.

38 Samuel Beckett, comment made to Alec Reid, 10 February 1966.

39 See Phyllis Gaffney, *Healing Amid the Ruins. The Irish Hospital at Saint-Lô (1945–46)* (Dublin: A. & A. Farmar, 1999).

40 Samuel Beckett, *Happy Days* (London: Faber & Faber, 1973), p. 19.

41 For an account of an occasion in Germany in 1937 when Beckett was well and truly 'conned', see James Knowlson, *Damned to Fame. The Life of Samuel Beckett* (London: Bloomsbury, 1996), pp. 254–6.

42 Samuel Beckett, *Disjecta. Miscellaneous Writings and a Dramatic Fragment* (London: John Calder, 1983), p. 52 (in German) and p. 171 (in English).

43 ibid., p. 94.

44 ibid., p. 171.

45 Samuel Beckett, interview with Tom Driver, *Columbia University Forum*, summer 1961, pp. 21–5, quoted in Lawrence Graver and Raymond Federman (ed.), *Samuel Beckett: The Critical Heritage* (London and New York: Routledge and Kegan Paul, 1979), p. 219.

46 The best account of Beckett's aesthetic development over the period 1930–53 is to be found in John Pilling, *Beckett Before Godot* (Cambridge: Cambridge University Press, 1997).

47 Samuel Beckett, interview with Gabriel d'Aubarède, *Nouvelles Littéraires*, 16 February 1961, quoted in Graver and Federman, *Beckett: The Critical Heritage*, p. 217.

48 Samuel Beckett, interview with James Knowlson, 27 October 1989.

49 Samuel Beckett, *Collected Shorter Plays* (London: Faber & Faber, 1984), p. 230.

50 SB, German Diaries, vol. 4, 15 January 1937.

IMAGES OF BECKETT

1 SB, letter to Alan Schneider, 16 October 1972. Maurice Harmon (ed.), *No Author Better Served: The Correspondence of Samuel Beckett and Alan Schneider* (Cambridge, MA: Harvard University Press, 1998), p. 283.

2 Quoted in S. E. Gontarski, *The Intent of Undoing in Samuel Beckett's Dramatic Texts* (Bloomington, IN: Indiana University Press, 1985), p. 214.

3 Beckett, *Collected Shorter Plays*, p. 242.

4 On Beckett and Nauman, see the fine catalogue of an exhibition staged at the Kunsthalle in Vienna, February–April 2000, entitled *Samuel Beckett Bruce Nauman*.

5 Werner Spies, 'Image Afterwards: an After Word' in *Word and Image. Samuel Beckett and the Visual Text*, ed. Breon Mitchell and Lois Overbeck (Atlanta, GA: Emory University Press, 1999), p. 55.

6 Manuscript notes in 'Eté 56', notebook entitled 'Play Female Solo'. MS 1227/7/7/1, archive of the Beckett International Foundation, University of Reading.

7 For a fuller discussion of this common approach to language, see Linda Ben-Zvi, 'Samuel Beckett, Fritz Mauthner and the Limits of Language', *PMLA* 95, no. 2, March 1980, pp. 183–200.

8 Beckett, *Disjecta*, p. 172.

9 Jim Lewis, 'Beckett et la caméra', *Samuel Beckett, Revue d'Esthétique*, hors série 1990 (Paris: Editions Jean-Michel Place), p. 376.

10 Samuel Beckett, conversation with Lawrence Harvey, 6 April 1962 (Harvey notes, Dartmouth College).

11 Samuel Beckett, conversation with Lawrence Harvey, 19 March 1962 (Harvey notes, Dartmouth College).

12 Anita Brookner to Boyd Tonkin, 'You Should Play Russian Roulette with Your Life', *Independent Magazine*, 29 June 2002.

13 Marin Karmitz, interview with Elisabeth Lebovici, in Marin Karmitz, *Samuel Beckett, Comédie* (Paris: Editions du Regard, 2001), p. 19 (in French), pp. 72–3 (in English).

14 Samuel Beckett, conversation with Lawrence Harvey, 7 November 1962 (Harvey notes, Dartmouth College).

15 Luke Gibbons and Kevin Whelan, 'In Conversation with Stephen Rea', 2 February 2001, *Yale Journal of Criticism* 15, no. 1, 2002, p. 6.

16 Beatrice Lady Glenavy, *Today We Will Only Gossip* (London: Constable, 1964), p. 178.

17 James Knowlson, *Damned to Fame. The Life of Samuel Beckett*, pp. 406–7.

18 Dougald McMillan and James Knowlson (eds.), *The Theatrical Notebooks of Samuel Beckett*, vol. 1, *Waiting for Godot* (London: Faber & Faber and New York: Grove Press, 1993), p. 238 [notebook p. 30].

19 SB, letter to James Knowlson, 28 April 1973.

20 Beckett, *Collected Shorter Plays*, p. 215.

21 For a discussion of an earlier attempt to write something for a 'severed-head image' called 'Kilcool', see Gontarski, *Intent of Undoing*, pp. 113–14, 133–42.

22 Copies of these six volumes of German diaries are now placed in the archive of the Beckett International Foundation at the University of Reading.

23 These various writings on art are usefully collected in *Proust and Three Dialogues with Georges Duthuit and Cohn (ed.), Disjecta*.

24 Samuel Beckett, *Murphy* (London: Calder & Boyars, 1969; 1st edition, 1938), p. 172.

25 Samuel Beckett, interview with James Knowlson, July 1989.

26 SB, letter to Tom MacGreevy, 8 September 1934.

27 Avigdor Arikha, undated personal conversation with James Knowlson.

28 'The Giorgione [*Venus Sleeping* in Dresden's Gemäldegalerie] is in a mess. The putto with the arrow and the bright bird sitting at her feet (by Giorgione or Titian?) was painted over with senseless landscape in the 19th century and the whole line of the left leg

destroyed.' SB, letter to Tom MacGreevy, 16 February 1937.

29 'Wonderful Signorellis especially the big Pan as God of Nature and Master of Music, with a shepherd very like the El Greco son of Laocoon in London.' SB, letter to Tom MacGreevy, 18 January 1937.

30 The two paintings, apparently done from a photograph, *Child at Prayer* and *Twins*, are reproduced in Marjorie Reynolds, *'Everything You Do is a Portrait of Yourself'. Dorothy Kay: A Biography* (Cape Town: Carrefour Press, 1989), p. 14, and in Marjorie Reynolds (ed.), *The Elvery Family: A Memory. Memoirs of the Artist Dorothy Elvery* (Cape Town: Carrefour Press, 1991), pp. 37 and 41.

31 Beckett loved this little Brouwer painting when he was a student but clearly changed his mind about it a little later, writing in a letter: 'The Brouwer here is not so good as I used to think. Also it is very dirty.' SB, letter to Tom MacGreevy, 15 May 1935. But his enthusiasm for the Flemish painter remained with him all his life.

32 SB, German Diaries, vol. 4, 5 February 1937.

33 For a fuller account of Beckett's relations with the Sinclairs and especially with their daughter, Peggy, see Knowlson, *Damned to Fame*, pp. 79–86, 108–10, 168–9.

34 For information on the modern paintings belonging to William Sinclair that Beckett saw in Kassel, I rely on interviews with Samuel Beckett July–November 1989, conversations with and letters from Sinclair's son, Morris, and the manuscript of a lecture on modern German art that William Sinclair gave in Dublin on his return to Ireland.

35 Samuel Beckett, *Dream of Fair to Middling Women* (Dublin: Black Cat Press, 1992), p. 77.

36 Some lists of paintings that Beckett saw in the various London galleries have been preserved in the archive of the Beckett International Foundation at the University of Reading.

37 Beckett, *More Pricks than Kicks*, p. 93.

38 SB, letter to Tom MacGreevy, 2 December 1931.

39 Beckett, *More Pricks than Kicks*, p. 47.

40 Beckett, *Dream of Fair to Middling Women*, p. 174.

41 Quoted in Hersh Zeifman, 'Religious Imagery in the Plays of Samuel Beckett' in Ruby Cohn (ed.), *Samuel Beckett. A Collection of Criticism* (New York: MacGraw Hill, 1975), p. 93.

42 The trio may call to mind, for example, Giovanni Bellini's *The Dead Christ with Angels*, or a late sixteenth-century Procaccini picture on the same theme that Beckett had seen in the National Gallery of London on his many visits since 1932.

43 SB, letter to Tom MacGreevy, 9 January 1936.

44 Untitled manuscript of an unpublished play in French, MS 1227/7/16/2. Archive of the Beckett International Foundation, University of Reading.

45 Samuel Beckett, 'Enueg II' in *Collected Poems in English and French* (London: John Calder, 1977), p. 13.

46 George Herbert, 'The Sacrifice' in *The Temple, The Works of George Herbert in Prose and Verse* (London: Frederick Warne, n.d.), pp. 71–80.

47 For a fuller discussion, see Zeifman, 'Religious Imagery', pp. 85–94.

48 SB, German Diaries, vol. 4, 1 February 1937. Beckett could still remember Antonello's famous painting of Saint Sebastian over a decade later. He wrote that it was 'formidable, formidable. C'était dans la première salle, j'en étais bloqué chaque fois [Wonderful, wonderful. It was in the first room. I had to stop there every time].' SB, letter to Georges Duthuit, 27 July 1948.

49 For a discussion of the Saint Veronica handkerchief in the context of *Nacht und Träume*, see Graley Herren, 'Splitting Images: Samuel Beckett's *Nacht und Träume*', *Modern Drama* 43, no. 2, 2000, pp. 182–91.

50 Information from Beckett's cousin, Morris Sinclair.

51 Graley Herren, '*Nacht und Träume* as Beckett's *Agony in the Garden*', *Journal of Beckett Studies* 11, no. 1, spring 2001, pp. 54–70.

52 Zeifman, 'Religious Imagery', p. 94.

53 SB, German Diaries, vol. 3, 5 January 1937: 'Interesting very early *Geldwechster* (1627), apparently influenced by Honthorst. One aspect of Rembrandt is nothing but a development of Honthorst.'

54 Chr. Tümpel, *Jahrbuch der Hamburger Kunstsammlungen* 16, 1971, pp. 27ff.

55 Luke 12:16–21.

56 Samuel Beckett, *Eh Joe and Other Writings* (London: Faber & Faber, 1967), p. 19: 'Thou fool thy soul'.

57 Atik, *How It Was*, p. 6.

58 Beckett, *More Pricks than Kicks*, p. 190.

59 John Pilling, *Beckett's Dream Notebook* (Reading: Beckett International Foundation, University of Reading, 1999), pp. 104–40 (Robert Burton). The quotations from Dante refer to the Provençal poet, Sordello, and are taken from the *Purgatorio*, canto 6, lines 57 and 72. The latter phrase actually reads 'tutta in se romita' in Dante and is translated by Cary as '[the shadow,] in itself absorbed'. Cary's note quotes Monti's remark that this does not mean 'solitary' but 'collected, concentrated in itself'. Henry Francis Cary, *The Vision; or, Hell, Purgatory and Paradise of Dante Alighieri* (author's corrected edition) (London: Bell and Daldy, 1869), p. 82, n. 6. The last phrase would characterise many of Beckett's own stage figures.

60 Beckett, *More Pricks than Kicks*, p. 190. The very similar passage in *Dream of Fair to Middling Women* is found on p. 15 of the Black Cat Press edition (Dublin, 1992).

61 'Interview with Billie Whitelaw by James Knowlson', *Journal of Beckett Studies* no. 3, summer 1978, p. 89.

62 William Cunningham, Radio Telefís Éireann, first broadcast, April 1976.

63 Lecture notes of Grace West (née McKinley), deposited in the archive of the Beckett International Foundation, University of Reading.

64 Among other paintings, I think of Dürer's *The Virgin in Prayer* in the Gemäldegalerie in Berlin.

65 Billie Whitelaw, *Billie Whitelaw . . . Who He?* (London: Hodder & Stoughton, 1995), p. 144.

66 Michael Haerdter's rehearsal diary in Dougald McMillan and Martha Fehsenfeld, *Beckett in the Theatre* (London: John Calder; and New York: Riverrun Press, 1988), p. 211.

67 Samuel Beckett, *Krapp's Last Tape and Embers* (London: Faber & Faber, 1959), pp. 16, 18.

68 SB, letter to Tom MacGreevy, 20 February [1935].

69 R. H. Wilenski, *An Introduction to Dutch Art* (London: Faber & Faber, 1929). The discussion of spotlight painting appears in the pages on the paintings of Elsheimer and Honthorst. Beckett's thirty-five pages of notes on Wilenski are preserved in Trinity College Library and the archive of the Beckett International Foundation at the University of Reading.

70 SB, letter to Tom MacGreevy, 20 February [1935].

71 Beckett, *Collected Shorter Plays*, p. 239.

72 Beckett's German Diaries, vol. 3, 5 January 1937.

73 Wilenski, *Introduction to Dutch Art*, facing p. 261.

74 See Damian Love, 'Beckett and the Romantik. The Art of Caspar David Friedrich', *Journal of Beckett Studies* 9, no. 2, spring 2000, pp. 91–6.

75 Whitelaw, *Billie Whitelaw . . . Who He?*, p. 145.

76 [Samuel Beckett], 'Recent Irish Poetry', in Cohn (ed.), *Disjecta*, p. 70.

77 SB, letter to Tom MacGreevy, 8 September 1934.

78 ibid.

79 ibid.

80 Beckett used this term in his article 'Recent Irish Poetry' in Cohn (ed.), *Disjecta*, p. 70 and again in this passage of his German Diaries: 'Interesting notes in Marc [Franz Marc, the German Expressionist painter] re subject, predicate, object relations in painting. He says: *paint the predicate of the living, Picasso has that of the inanimate.* By that he appears to mean not the *relation* between subject & object, but the *alienation* (my nomansland). The object *particularizes, banalizes* the "thought" which

fires me: *Musik ist Satz ohne Objekt.*' SB, German Diaries, vol. 2, 19 November 1936.

81 SB, letter to Tom MacGreevy, 14 August 1937. The painting to which Beckett refers here is Jack B. Yeats' *The Storm*, painted in 1936.

82 SB, letter to Georges Duthuit, 2 March 1954.

83 Beckett, *Proust and Three Dialogues with Georges Duthuit*, p. 66.

84 Samuel Beckett, *Waiting for Godot* (London: Faber & Faber, 1985), p. 61.

85 Beckett, *Collected Shorter Plays*, p. 241.

86 'I have a queer lot of pictures here now. A German surrealist called Paalen gave me some kind of "automatic" affair that amuses me, and I have started paying for a picture by a Polish Jew called Adler that I like very much.' SB, letter to Tom MacGreevy, 18 April 1939.

87 'I went to Otto Freundlich's exhibition at Jeanne Bucher's. A subscription list has been opened to buy a picture and present it to the Jeu de Paume . . . The picture in question is a very fine one, far and away the best in the show. There is also a very beautiful sculpture in the little garden in front of the gallery. I met him once a couple of months ago and found him very sympathetic.' SB to Tom MacGreevy, 15 June 1938.

88 Joan Mitchell (1926–92), an abstract expressionist painter, born in Chicago, who lived in France from 1959, first in Paris and then in Vétheil. For many years she was the partner of the Canadian abstract painter, Jean-Paul Riopelle. See Jane Livingston, *The Paintings of Joan Mitchell*, with essays by Linda Nochlin and Yvette Lee (Berkeley, CA: University of California Press, 2002). Riopelle (b. 1923) was influenced by Kandinsky, Miró and Pollock. For Riopelle's life, see Hélène de Billy, *Riopelle* (Montreal: Editions Art Global, 1996), and for his painting see Pierre Schneider, *Riopelle signes mêlés* (Paris: Maeght Editeur, 1972).

89 'Begin to get slightly tired of S.R.'s [Schmidt-Rottluff's] determination to see big, there is a programmatic

monumentalism that does not justify its simplifications. But a lovely coloured drawing of a woman looking at a picture. I find Kirchner a purer artist, incredible line and sureness of taste and fineness of colour.' SB, German Diaries, vol. 3, 19 December 1936.

90 SB, German Diaries, vol. 2, 23 January 1937.

91 He saw, for instance, Munch's painting *Einsamkeit* (*Loneliness*), still hanging on the walls of the Kronprinzenpalais in Berlin, as 'lovely, woman in red doublet up on blue stool, rainbow coloured heap on left (bathing tent?), and pale unlimited motionless emptiness of sea'. But his sometime problems with Munch remained: he wrote of this particular painting, 'But even here the feeling inclined to be overstated into the sentimental . . . The *Krankes Mädchen* drawing also only just over the pretty line. What is it in this uncompromising *Norderin* [?] (*Nolde & Hamsun* also – Albrecht [with whom Beckett was friendly in Hamburg] was an admirer of Hamsun) – that always threatens to upset the whole apple-cart. It is in the German Gothic also, more than in the English.' SB, German Diaries, vol. 4, 20 January 1937.

92 Daniel Albright, 'Beckett as Marsyas' in Lois Oppenheim (ed.), *Samuel Beckett and the Arts. Music, Visual Art and Non-Print Media* (New York and London: Garland, 1999), pp. 25–49.

93 SB, German Diaries, vol. 2, 23 January 1937.

94 Beckett, *Collected Shorter Plays*, p. 228.

95 ibid., p. 216.

96 See Enoch Brater, *Why Beckett* (London: Thames & Hudson, 1989), pp. 29 and 100.

97 SB, German Diaries, vol. 1, 4 November 1936.

98 Michaël Glasmeier and Gaby Hartel, 'Three Grey Disks, Comédie' in Marin Karmitz, *Samuel Beckett, Comédie*, pp. 33–4 (in French), p. 82 (in English).

99 Samuel Beckett, 'MacGreevy on Yeats' in Cohn (ed.), *Disjecta*, p. 97.

100 John Gruen, 'Samuel Beckett Talks About Samuel Beckett', *Vogue* 154, no. 10, December 1969, p. 210.

101 Samuel Beckett, *Lessness* (London: Calder & Boyars, 1970), Signature series 9, back cover, extract of the blurb written by Beckett himself.

102 ibid., p. 7.

103 Samuel Beckett, *Worstward Ho* (London: John Calder, 1983), p. 13.

104 ibid., p. 45.

105 ibid., pp. 28 and 33.

106 Marin Karmitz, interview with Elisabeth Lebovici in Marin Karmitz Samuel Beckett, *Comédie*, p. 20 (in French), p. 73 (in English).

BECKETT AS DIRECTOR

1 One notable instance was the Schiller Theatre production, directed by the dancer Deryk Mendel in February 1965, when Beckett came in, albeit reluctantly, at the request of the Schiller Theatre's dramaturg to help Mendel out.

2 That Suzanne Beckett gave her husband detailed reports on productions she went to see on his behalf is clear from Beckett's letter to Alan Schneider of 26 November 1963 about Mendel's German production of *Play* in Berlin. See Harmon (ed.), *No Author Better Served*, pp. 144–6.

3 Michael Haerdter's rehearsal diary in McMillan and Fehsenfeld, *Beckett in the Theatre*, p. 230.

4 Beckett attended six performances of Peter Hall's production of *Waiting for Godot* at the Criterion Theatre in London in the winter of 1955.

5 Alan Schneider, *Entrances. An American Director's Journey* (New York: Viking Penguin, 1986), p. 225.

6 Beckett's letter to Peter Hall of 14 December 1955 and his suggestions after seeing the Criterion Theatre production are printed in Harmon (ed.), *No Author Better Served*, pp. 2–5.

7 Haerdter's rehearsal diary, in McMillan and Fehsenfeld, *Beckett in the Theatre*, p. 230.

8 Harmon (ed.), *No Author Better Served*, p. 59. In the same vein, Beckett wrote of the production by Deryk Mendel in Ulm, Donau, 'It will be a very careful and conscientious production, without more, but at least no director's improvements, which is a rare thing in Germany.' SB, letter to Henry Wenning, 10 June 1963.

9 Ruby Cohn, *Just Play: Beckett's Theater* (Princeton, NJ: Princeton University Press, 1980), p. 258.

10 Harmon (ed.), *No Author Better Served*, p. 144. The text of *Play* was in fact revised after Beckett had worked on the 1964 Paris and London productions.

11 Haerdter's rehearsal diary, in McMillan and Fehsenfeld, *Beckett in the Theatre*, p. 207.

12 Walter Asmus, 'Beckett Directs Beckett', *Theatre Quarterly* 5, no. 19, 1975, p. 26.

13 Whitelaw, *Billie Whitelaw . . . Who He?*, p. 153.

14 McMillan and Fehsenfeld, *Beckett in the Theatre*, p. 177.

15 Harmon (ed.), *No Author Better Served*, p. 23.

16 McMillan and Fehsenfeld, *Beckett in the Theatre*, p. 204.

17 Haerdter's rehearsal diary, ibid., p. 212.

18 Clancy Sigal, 'Is This the Person to Murder Me?', *Sunday Times* (colour magazine), 1 March 1964, reprinted as 'Rehearsal Diary' of the Aldwych Theatre, London production in McMillan and Fehsenfeld, *Beckett in the Theatre*, p. 179.

19 Haerdter's rehearsal diary in McMillan and Fehsenfeld, *Beckett in the Theatre*, p. 208.

20 Alfred Hübner, *Samuel Beckett inszeniert 'Glückliche Tage', Probenprotokoll von Alfred Hübner* (Frankfurt: Suhrkamp Verlag, 1976), pp. 38–9.

21 Beckett's comment was recorded by Martha Fehsenfeld.

22 Rick Cluchey in an unpublished memoir entitled 'From the Dead'.

23 Haerdter's rehearsal diary, in McMillan and Fehsenfeld, *Beckett in the Theatre*, p. 228.

24 ibid., p. 238.

25 Schneider, *Entrances*, p. 224.

26 For examples of Beckett's knowledge of and passion for poetry see Atik, *How It Was*, passim.

27 SB, German Diaries, vol. 4, 12 January 1937.

28 SB, letter to Mary Manning, 18 January 1937.

29 SB, German Diaries, vol. 4, 12 January 1937.

30 Beckett, *Waiting for Godot*, p. 89.

31 ibid., p. 62.

32 Since completing this essay, I found an interesting discussion of Beckett and Craig in Jennifer M. Jeffers' recent book, *Uncharted Space: The End of Narrative, Literature and the Visual Arts New Foundations* 15 (New York: Peter Lang, 2001).

33 Edward Gordon Craig, *The Art of the Theatre* (Edinburgh and London: T. N. Fouhis, 1911), pp. 17–18.

34 SB, letter to James Knowlson, 11 April 1972.

35 Antonin Artaud, *The Theatre and its Double*, Signature 4 (London: John Calder, 1977), p. 27.

36 ibid., p. 33.

37 Jean Cocteau, *Théâtre*, vol. 1, preface to *Les Mariés de la Tour Eiffel* (Paris: Gallimard, 1948), p. 45.

38 Denis Bablet, *The Theatre of Edward Gordon Craig*, trans. Daphne Woodward (London: Eyre Methuen, 1981), p. 108.

39 David Bradby, *Waiting for Godot*, Plays in Production (Cambridge: Cambridge University Press, 2001), p. 133.

40 Asmus, 'Beckett Directs Beckett', p. 23.

41 Haerdter's rehearsal diary, in McMillan and Fehsenfeld, *Beckett in the Theatre*, p. 205.

42 James Knowlson (ed.), *Happy Days: Samuel Beckett's Production Notebook* (London: Faber & Faber, 1985), p. 16. The quotations here are taken from a rehearsal diary kept by Martha Fehsenfeld.

43 Craig, *Art of the Theatre*, preface p. 37, quoted in Bablet, *Theatre of Edward Gordon Craig*, p. 109.

44 ibid.

45 Extracts from the interview with Siân Phillips are printed in Knowlson, *Damned to Fame*, p. 538.

46 For a fuller discussion of Beckett's reading of Kleist's Marionette essay, see James Knowlson and John Pilling, *Frescoes of the Skull. The Later Prose and Drama of Samuel Beckett* (London: John Calder, 1979), pp. 277–85.

47 Whitelaw, *Billie Whitelaw . . . Who He?*, p. 152.

48 Stuart Burge, letter to James Knowlson, 23 March 1993.

49 John Goodwin (ed.), *Peter Hall's Diaries. The Story of a Dramatic Battle* (London: Hamish Hamilton, 1983), p. 127.

50 These one-to-one conversations with Dame Peggy Ashcroft and Samuel Beckett took place at the time when *Happy Days* was being rehearsed at the Old Vic Theatre, London, in October 1974.

51 SB, letter to Alan Schneider, 4 January 1960. 'I told you about the beautiful and quite accidental effect in London of the luminous eye burning up as the machine runs on in silence and the light goes down.' Harmon (ed.), *No Author Better Served*, p. 59.

52 SB, undated letter to James Knowlson.

53 Haerdter's rehearsal diary, in McMillan and Fehsenfeld, *Beckett in the Theatre*, p. 211.

54 S. E. Gontarski (ed.), *The Theatrical Notebooks of Samuel Beckett*, vol. II, *Endgame* (London: Faber & Faber and New York: Grove Press, 1992), p. xix.

55 SB, letter to Tom MacGreevy, 6 February 1936.

56 SB, letter to Tom MacGreevy, 29 January 1936.

57 SB, letter to Tom MacGreevy, 25 March 1936.

58 Beckett's letter to Eisenstein was published in Jay Leyda, *Eisenstein 2: A Premature Celebration of Eisenstein's Centenary*, trans. Alan Y. Upchurch, N. Lary, Zina Voynow and Samuel Brody (Calcutta: Seagull Books, 1985), p. 59.

59 For an account of Joyce's meetings with Eisenstein, see Ronald Bargan, *Sergei Eisenstein. A Life in Conflict* (Woodstock and New York: Overlook Press, 1999), p. 185.

60 SB, letter to Tom MacGreevy, 6 February 1936.

61 SB, letter to Tom MacGreevy, 11 February 1938.

62 SB, letter to Tom MacGreevy, 25 March 1936.

63 In the story 'The Smeraldina's Billet Doux', Beckett has the writer of the love letter from Germany write in her fractured English: 'I was at a grand Film last night, first of all there wasent any of the usual hugging and kissing, I think I have never enjoyed or felt so sad at a Film as that one, Sturm uber Asien, if it comes to Dublin you must go and see it, the same regie as Der Lebende Leichnam, it was realey something quite different from all other Films, nothing to do with Love (as everybody understands the word) no silly girls makeing sweet faces, black lakes and grand Landschaften.' *More Pricks than Kicks*, p. 163.

64 Rudolf Arnheim, *Film*, trans. from the German by L. M. Sieveking and Ian F. D. Morrow, with a preface by Paul Rotha (London: Faber & Faber, 1933), pp. 102–3.

65 When the topic of Beckett and film has been discussed, critics have tended to focus on the impact of Eisenstein, for example, an interesting paper given by Lois Overbeck at a Beckett Conference in Strasbourg in 1996, later entitled 'Through the Aperture: Film, Television and Samuel Beckett'. While in no way underestimating the impact of Beckett's reading of Eisenstein's theoretical essays and of Pudovkin, his reading of Arnheim's book seems to me to be of greater importance.

66 Arnheim, *Film*, p. 102.

67 ibid., p. 103.

68 Beckett, *Krapp's Last Tape and Embers*, p. 14.

69 Arnheim, *Film*, p. 77.

70 Mary Bryden, Julian Garforth and Peter Mills (eds.), *Beckett at Reading. Catalogue of the Beckett Manuscript Collection at The University of Reading* (Reading: Whiteknights Press and Beckett International Foundation, 1998), p. 94.

71 For details of this related patterning see S. E. Gontarski (ed.), *The Theatrical Notebooks of Samuel Beckett*, vol. IV, *The Shorter Plays* (London: Faber & Faber, 1999), pp. 386 and 394.

72 The brilliant film of this play made by Anthony Minghella in 2001 for the Beckett on Film project illustrates particularly well the affinity between Beckett's writing and montage. Minghella's editor has provided an astounding example of inter-cutting with variety and speed.

73 J. M. B. Antoine-Dunne, 'Beckett and Eisenstein on Light and Contrapuntal Montage' in *Samuel Beckett: Endlessness in the Year 2000. Samuel Beckett: Fin sans fin en l'an 2000. Samuel Beckett Today/Aujourd'hui*, ed. Angela Moorjani and Carola Veit (Amsterdam, New York: Rodopi, 2001), pp. 315–30.

74 ibid., p. 316.

75 ibid.

76 Harmon (ed.), *No Author Better Served*, p. 283.

77 Samuel Beckett, *Endgame* (London: Faber & Faber 1972), p. 35.

78 Gontarski (ed.), *Theatrical Notebooks of Samuel Beckett*, vol. II, *Endgame*, p. xx.

79 Arnheim, *Film*, p. 110.

80 ibid.

81 ibid., pp. 120–1.

82 ibid., p. 110.

83 ibid., p. 121.

84 V. I. Pudovkin, *Film Technique. Five Essays and Two Addresses*, translated and annotated by Ivor Montagu, enlarged edition (London: George Newnes, 1933), p. 65.

85 Haerdter's rehearsal diary, in McMillan and Fehsenfeld, *Beckett in the Theatre*, p. 216.

86 Samuel Beckett, interview with Charles Marowitz, *Encore* 9, March–April 1962, pp. 43–5.

87 His cousin, Morris Sinclair, wrote recently of Beckett's visits to his home: 'Sam, in his visits to the Sinclairs in Kassel, brought in something musically new, at least to me. He played Granados, and, as I remember, gave

passionate renderings of Mozart's A minor sonata and the last movement of Beethoven's early C minor sonata.' Letter to James Knowlson, 17 May 2002. Included among the sheet music left after his death in his country house in Ussy (where he still had a piano) were Beethoven's opus 109, Sonata 32, opus 11 and Variations for the piano; Schubert's Impromptus and Sonatas; Haydn's Sonatas, Clavierstücke and Andante con variatione in F minor; Chopin's Waltzes and Sonatas; Bartók's Microcosmos; as well as other Mozart, Beethoven and Chopin piano music from his childhood.

88 Haerdter's rehearsal diary, in McMillan and Fehsenfeld, *Beckett in the Theatre*, p. 226.

89 Whitelaw, *Billie Whitelaw . . . Who He?* pp. 151 and 174.

90 The original unchanged text is quoted from Beckett, *Happy Days*, p. 20. Beckett's revised text is given in Knowlson (ed.), *Happy Days: Samuel Beckett's Production Notebook*, p. 193.

91 Beckett, *Happy Days*, p. 45.

92 McMillan and Knowlson (eds.), *Theatrical Notebooks of Samuel Beckett*, vol. I, *Waiting for Godot*, pp. 185–7.

93 Beckett, *Waiting for Godot*, p. 15.

94 Haerdter's rehearsal diary, in McMillan and Fehsenfeld, *Beckett in the Theatre*, p. 236.

95 ibid.

96 Beckett, *Waiting for Godot*, p. 11.

97 ibid.

98 The detailed changes and echoes are all recorded in Gontarski's edition of *The Theatrical Notebooks of Samuel Beckett*, vol. II, *Endgame*.

99 James Knowlson (ed.), *The Theatrical Notebooks of Samuel Beckett*, vol. III, *Krapp's Last Tape* (London: Faber & Faber, 1992), p. 217.

100 ibid., p. 101.

101 Peter Hall, 'Sincerely Sam', *Observer*, 14 February 1999, p. 13.

102 These comments were recorded at rehearsals at the Royal Court by James Knowlson and Martha Fehsenfeld.

103 Haerdter's rehearsal diary in McMillan and Fehsenfeld, *Beckett in the Theatre*, p. 236.

104 Knowlson (ed.), *Theatrical Notebooks of Samuel Beckett*, vol. III, *Krapp's Last Tape*, p. 101.

105 ibid., p. 157.

106 Asmus, 'Beckett Directs Beckett', pp. 21 and 22.

107 Knowlson (ed.), *Theatrical Notebooks of Samuel Beckett*, vol. I, *Waiting for Godot*, p. 14, and introduction, p. xiv.

108 Preliminary Schiller Theatre notebook, MS 1396/4/3, facing p. 1, archive of the Beckett International Foundation, University of Reading.

109 ibid.

110 James Knowlson (ed.), *Samuel Beckett 'Krapp's Last Tape'* (London: Brutus Books, 1980), p. 127.

111 Walter Asmus, 'Practical Aspects of Theatre, Radio and Television: Rehearsal Notes for the German Première of Beckett's *That Time* and *Footfalls* at the Schiller-Theater Werkstatt, Berlin', *Journal of Beckett Studies* no. 2, summer 1977, p. 91.

112 Hübner, *Samuel Beckett inszeniert 'Glückliche Tage'*, pp. 38–9.

113 Beckett, *Happy Days*, pp. 26 and 29.

114 Samuel Beckett, manuscript notes on histories of philosophy in Trinity College, Dublin, and at the archive of the Beckett International Foundation, University of Reading.

115 Knowlson (ed.), *Happy Days: Samuel Beckett's Production Notebook*, p. 87 [notebook entry p. 37].

116 ibid., pp. 118–19 [notebook entry p. 53].

117 ibid., p. 185.

118 Hübner, *Samuel Beckett inszeniert 'Glückliche Tage'*.

119 Knowlson (ed.), *Happy Days: Samuel Beckett's Production Notebook*, p. 150.

120 Beckett, *Happy Days*, p. 38.

121 Beckett, *Endgame*, p. 12.

122 Gontarski (ed.), *Theatrical Notebooks of Beckett*, vol. II, *Endgame*, pp. 195–7.

123 ibid., pp. 191–3.

124 Beckett, *Endgame*, pp. 23–4.

125 Beckett's notes were published in Knowlson (ed.), *Theatrical Notebooks of Samuel Beckett*, vol. III, *Krapp's Last Tape*.

126 SB, letter to James Knowlson, 19 April 1972.

127 Harmon (ed.), *No Author Better Served*, p. 60.

128 Arnheim, *Film*, p. 77. Arnheim gave another example that is interesting in the light of Beckett's own use of light and dark images in *Krapp's Last Tape*. 'In Granowsky's "Song of Life" the emotional scene in the operating theatre achieves its terrifying silence and harshness by the pictorial contrast between the long white operating coats, the white sterile sheets, the white cottonwool, and the dark rubber gloves of the doctors with their dark instruments' (p. 78).

129 Edith Fournier, 'Marcel Mihalovici and Samuel Beckett: Musicians of Return' in Mary Bryden (ed.), *Samuel Beckett and Music* (Oxford: Clarendon Press), p. 135.

130 Samuel Beckett, 'German Letter of 1937', *Disjecta*, English translation by Martin Esslin, p. 172.

131 ibid.

132 Beckett's comment is quoted in the afterword to John Fletcher's edition of *Waiting for Godot* (London: Faber & Faber, 1971), p. 120.

Index